T0319602

CAMPUS ECONOMICS

Campus Economics

HOW ECONOMIC THINKING CAN HELP IMPROVE COLLEGE AND UNIVERSITY DECISIONS

Sandy Baum

Michael McPherson

PRINCETON UNIVERSITY PRESS

PRINCETON & OXFORD

Published by Princeton University Press
41 William Street, Princeton, New Jersey 08540
99 Banbury Road, Oxford OX2 6JX

press.princeton.edu

All Rights Reserved

Library of Congress Cataloging-in-Publication Data

Names: Baum, Sandy (Sandra R.), author. | McPherson, Michael S., author.
Title: Campus economics : how economic thinking can help improve college and university decisions / Sandy Baum, Michael McPherson.
Description: Princeton, New Jersey : Princeton University Press, 2023. | Includes bibliographical references and index.
Identifiers: LCCN 2022013087 (print) | LCCN 2022013088 (ebook) | ISBN 9780691229928 (hardcover) | ISBN 9780691229935 (ebook)
Subjects: LCSH: Universities and colleges—United States—Finance. | Universities and colleges—United States—Administration—Decision making. | BISAC: EDUCATION / Schools / Levels / Higher | BUSINESS & ECONOMICS / General
Classification: LCC LB2342 .B368 2023 (print) | LCC LB2342 (ebook) | DDC 378.1/06—dc23/eng/20220510
LC record available at https://lccn.loc.gov/2022013087
LC ebook record available at https://lccn.loc.gov/2022013088

British Library Cataloging-in-Publication Data is available

Editorial: Peter Dougherty, Alena Chekanov
Production Editorial: Terri O'Prey
Jacket Design: Heather Hansen
Production: Erin Suydam
Publicity: James Schneider, Kathryn Stevens
Copyeditor: Michele Rosen

This book has been composed in Miller

Printed on acid-free paper. ∞

Printed in the United States of America

10 9 8 7 6 5 4 3 2 1

CONTENTS

ACKNOWLEDGMENTS

WE ARE GRATEFUL to our Princeton University Press editor, Peter Dougherty, for encouraging us to write this book and providing advice that strengthened our work. Mary Clark, Francesca Purcell, Kevin Reilly, Morton Schapiro, and Sarah Turner provided helpful comments on earlier drafts. And we have both learned a tremendous amount from a wide range of people over the course of our careers, making this project possible.

CAMPUS ECONOMICS

Introduction

MOST COLLEGES AND UNIVERSITIES, with the likely exception of for-profit institutions, see themselves as motivated by a mission beyond simply staying in business and making money. The idea that the members of a campus community share a purpose or set of purposes leads naturally to the idea that everyone who participates in that community should have a voice in how that mission is pursued.

On some campuses, the model of shared governance provides meaningful voice for multiple constituencies in institutional decision-making. Faculty and staff, and sometimes students, participate with administrators and trustees in deliberations over the challenges facing the college or university. At other institutions, the lines of responsibility are much more tightly drawn. But in all cases, decisions about how to further the mission, as well as about how to ensure financial strength, affect all members of the community.

Sometimes competing priorities make consensus difficult. But even in the presence of shared objectives, communication problems frequently make for difficult conversations. The goal of this book is to facilitate communication among groups on campus by creating a common vocabulary and encouraging modes of thinking that allow participants to better see other viewpoints and grapple with the trade-offs involved in making sound decisions.

How you see problems depends on where you sit. The same person with the same history and values may have different information and weigh facts differently depending on her current position and responsibilities. Moreover, participants come to the table with different backgrounds and experiences, different vocabularies, and different ways of analyzing situations.

The hope that inspired this book is that people in different positions with different responsibilities can exchange ideas, respecting each other's perspectives. Even if they cannot reach consensus, understanding each other's languages and communicating about their values and priorities can ease tensions, allow for decision makers to be influenced by differing views, and create a sense of a community with shared goals, even when decisions are controversial.

Shared governance does not make a college or university into a majority-rule democracy. Trustees have a legal and moral responsibility to ensure the long-term financial health of the institution. Faculty have expertise and experience that give their views special weight in matters of curriculum and in the hiring and retention of their colleagues. But a campus with shared governance is not a collection of fiefdoms, with each group ruling in its own sphere. Instead, an effective system of shared governance should help people understand how to coordinate the variety of responsibilities that make up the campus, enabling the whole operation to work well, with constructive deliberation across constituencies.

It is often difficult for people with expertise and responsibility to communicate effectively with others who don't share their vocabulary or their priorities. People who care passionately about their work and their communities may struggle to objectively evaluate options that are limited by choices over which they have had no control or by scarce resources. It is a challenge to be open to the idea that alternative perspectives may improve one's own judgments no matter how much experience and knowledge one has.

The authors of this book were longtime faculty members. We are both economists who have studied higher education for many years. Although our primary affiliations have been with liberal arts colleges,[1] we have also spent many years consulting with a wide variety of colleges and universities and as advisors and analysts for a broad range of higher education associations, thinking deeply about many types of colleges and universities, from top research universities to the broad-access institutions that are especially important for students without strong academic preparation, particularly first-generation and low-income students. Over the years we have found this intellectual "travel" broadening. We have come to appreciate that institutions with different traditions, student bodies, and financial constraints in some ways live in different worlds, but that all these institutions have some kinds of problems in common. They must, for example, meet the financial demands of various programs and constituencies, help the students with the greatest need while attracting others who can help pay the bills, and understand what "success" is in their particular environment.

We have spent much of our careers communicating with non-economists about issues people see quite differently depending on whether their primary focus is social equity, fiscal responsibility, academic freedom, intellectual rigor, or another central aspect of the missions of higher education institutions.

As economists, we know how resistant many people are to the terminology of our discipline and how much they disagree with and fear the idea of allowing resource constraints to guide decisions about intellectual, ethical, or social issues. We also know how difficult many economists find it to make sense of values and concerns that don't translate easily into a cost-benefit calculus. We have learned (sometimes the hard way) that our favorite vocabulary and jargon (opportunity cost, marginal this and that, price elasticity of demand) can be more off-putting than enlightening. But we also know how valuable economic reasoning and concepts can be for analyzing a wide range of issues, many of which have little to do with money or material goods—and how inadequate these concepts can be if relied on exclusively or applied blindly. We are convinced that sharing concepts is a first step toward using them wisely and constructively.

Underlying all the discussion in this book is the conviction that the primary goal of campus decision-making is to further the institution's educational mission. There is no clear answer to many of the dilemmas that colleges face and certainly not one right answer that will fit all colleges and universities or even all similar institutions. But inadequate understanding of the fundamentals of institutional finances and the lack of a common language for debating the pros and cons of difficult decisions almost always add to the difficulty of reaching consensus on constructive solutions. A shared understanding of the facts and concepts will not eliminate differences in priorities or predictions about the future. But it will provide the basis for more constructive dialogue. Poor communication increases the likelihood of pursuing ineffective policies and strategies that diminish the chances of furthering the institutional mission.

Despite significant differences in the structure, missions, and financing of different types of higher education institutions, all must pursue their missions in the face of resource constraints, balancing short-term and long-term goals. This is true of both public and private institutions, of universities with broad missions including research and the education of graduate students, as well as of community colleges focused principally on the first years of postsecondary education. It is true of colleges and universities ranging from the most selective to those accepting all comers. The concepts and principles contained in these chapters should be useful for anyone faced with the reality of required trade-offs in an educational environment.

We have chosen a few specific examples of the choices facing institutions that might be facilitated by the type of analytical approach we encourage. Different issues will rise to the top or create the greatest controversy at different institutions and at different times. But the same tools will be relevant. Some of the issues we address gained prominence early in the pandemic, as colleges and universities saw revenues declining and expenditures rising while they were forced to pivot quickly to online operations. Others have been high priority items on institutional agendas for decades.

These issues illustrate matters that frequently create tensions on college campuses as well as in public discourse and policy conversations. There are many other problems that can benefit from a similar form of analysis. Very few campus issues should be viewed as purely economic in nature. College finances are supportive of the central educational mission, not the primary motivating factor. Nonetheless, the understanding and application of basic economic concepts can frequently raise the quality of debate on campus.

The issue-based chapters of this book focus on the following questions:

Is a college a business?

Discussions between faculty members and trustees—or other groups on campus—can easily be derailed by a fundamental difference in the way members of the community think and talk about the enterprise. Is it a business much like any other, striving to satisfy the demands of customers? Are increasing revenues, cutting expenditures, and adding to the endowment reliable measures of success? Should supply and demand determine salary structures? Under what circumstances should departments with small and declining enrollments be subsidized by those for which there is greater demand? Should decisions about the curriculum be separate from budgetary considerations? Should social justice priorities outweigh net revenue considerations in enrolling students and providing them with financial aid? These questions can elicit emotional reactions from many on campus. The tools we offer may bring different constituencies closer together as they wrestle with the choices these questions require.

How should we think about the compensation budget?

Controversies about cost-saving measures such as cutting contributions to employee retirement accounts and furloughing employees were center stage during the pandemic. Could budgets possibly be trimmed enough without cutting into this core of institutional expenditures? Is reducing employment a better alternative than cutting compensation levels? Should maintaining retirement contributions take precedence over salary increases? These issues are not easy to resolve.

Do we really have to cut the budget?

Looking at questions from multiple perspectives can lead people to re-examine their own conclusions. Before taking a side on where the budget should be cut—if it should be cut at all—it is helpful to pose a range of questions. Many issues, from deferring maintenance to cutting noninstructional expenses to freezing hiring, can benefit from this type of analysis. And increasing revenues is an alternative to cutting the budget in search of fiscal stability.

Can pricing and financial aid policies be more transparent?

Concerns about declines in enrollment because of the physical and financial impacts of the pandemic or because of longer-term demographic and geographical trends are particularly stressful at the most tuition-dependent institutions. Understanding the differences between need-based and non-need-based aid, combined with insights into the price-sensitivity of different groups of students and the relationship between discounts and net tuition revenues, provides a starting point for judgments about the most appropriate policies and practices.

What is the role of college endowments?

A small number of colleges and universities hold the vast majority of all endowment assets. For these privileged few, questions arise about whether it is really necessary to make difficult choices when circumstances are temporarily strained. Many more campuses have to debate whether or how much to increase temporarily the draw on the endowment during hard times. Shared understanding of the sources and role of endowments can inform these debates.

Before jumping into these campus issues in more detail, the first three chapters provide background for challenging conversations. Chapter 1 paints a picture of higher education institutions in the United States, their students, and the credentials they award. It also includes data on college prices, the financial aid available to students to help pay those prices, and the family incomes supporting those students. In chapter 2, we provide a brief economics lesson, defining terms—such as demand, opportunity cost, and price sensitivity—that are helpful in addressing issues that arise on campus, and providing examples of how they can be meaningful. Readers with a background in economics will already be familiar with those concepts but may not have thought about how they apply to the daily issues faced on campus. Chapter 3 provides a parallel introduction to concepts in college financing such as the discount rate and gross versus net tuition revenues. Financial officers and others with responsibility for ensuring the fiscal stability of their institutions will be familiar with the building blocks of college finance. But they may not always focus on the ways in which nonprofit academic institutions differ from for-profit companies producing a range of other goods and services.

The remainder of the book addresses specific campus issues—not attempting to provide solutions to the problems with which campus participants are grappling but discussing alternative ways of looking at questions and evidence to reach reasonable conclusions that everyone can understand.

Our aim is to strengthen and broaden understanding of concepts that can help all participants analyze the pros, cons, and trade-offs of difficult decisions and provide the basics of a common language for discussing and debating the many challenges institutions face.

The idea of our discussion is not to focus primarily on the bottom line or the dollars and cents of providing higher education, but to help frame judgments considering the interaction between resources and outcomes, the trade-offs involved in many campus decisions, and the differing perspectives of people with shared goals but different and, sometimes conflicting, roles, responsibilities, and priorities. Economic concepts and reasoning can help all involved to think about how even the clearest choices eliminate other options, about how marginal reductions in vital expenditures need not cause serious harm, and about how decisions affect different members of the community.

The COVID Crisis

Since March 2020, when colleges and universities sent their students home for what most people thought might be just a few weeks, questions about the financial costs of the pandemic, how institutions will manage, and what the impact will be on faculty, staff, and curriculum—in addition to students—have accumulated. By the time you are reading this, we hope that many of the answers will have become clearer, but the terrible consequences of the Delta variant, followed by the Omicron variant, and the persistent political issues regarding public health measures suggest that the crisis is far from over. COVID offers a good, if painful, opportunity to think about how to respond to a serious but hopefully temporary crisis, as well as a sizeable one-time inflow of funds to address that crisis.

In February 2021, the *Chronicle of Higher Education* estimated institutions lost an average of 14 percent of their revenues compared to the preceding year. Overall, state budget cuts, tuition freezes, lost dormitory revenues, and enrollment declines, combined with emergency expenses, added up to an estimated $183 billion: $85 billion in lost revenues, $24 billion for COVID-related expenses, and $74 billion in anticipated future decreases in state funding.[2]

Early on, many institutions had to make quick decisions about cutting expenses to make ends meet. Many froze salaries and hiring, cut back on contributions to retirement accounts, furloughed workers, and took other steps that made life harder for faculty and staff.

By March 2021, Congress had passed three COVID relief spending packages that, combined, allocated $69 billion in aid to postsecondary institutions—not enough to compensate for all the losses, but enough to take a significant bite out of them. And because budgets in many states have come through better than predicted, some public institutions will not face funding cuts as draconian as they had feared.

The allocation of federal funds to individual institutions depended on enrollment levels, with low-income students counting more than others and additional allotments for minority-serving institutions. Colleges and universities have one year after the final disbursement to spend their emergency relief funds. About half of the funds must go directly to students.[3]

What is the best way to spend the remainder of the money? Differences of opinion are inevitable. Covering the expenses directly associated with the pandemic, such as the transition to virtual learning, COVID testing, and physical accommodation on campus, is an obvious area, and Congress required that some funds go to monitoring and suppressing the spread of the coronavirus.

One challenge is that the federal funds represent a one-time infusion of cash. To the extent that they make up for lost revenues that will return to the annual budget once enrollment recovers, they should diminish the need for budget cuts. But they are unlikely to be adequate for spending increases that have long been at the top of the list.

Salary and benefit increases are not one-time expenses. A 1 percent increase in compensation requires extra funds for years to come. But many institutions reduced their contributions to retirement benefits and/or froze faculty salaries during the pandemic. If they had known in advance that they would have this "windfall" from the federal government, these steps might not have been necessary. Compensating faculty and staff for the salary sacrifice they were forced to make would be a reasonable approach to consider.

If the starting point is the pre-pandemic situation, the one-time federal funds won't cover a continuing increase in the budget. But these funds do call for rethinking the necessity for cuts the institution made that will have a lasting impact.

What will happen when the crisis is over, whether that means really stamping out the virus or reducing it to a permanent simmer? One camp asserts that "this changes everything"—COVID has forced us to rethink both teaching and learning and the economics of higher education. Others anticipate, with a sigh of relief, that we can now return to "business as usual." We hope that higher education institutions have learned some lessons from the pandemic. We have a more tangible sense of the strengths and limitations of online learning; we have more dramatic evidence of the large variations in the circumstances students face in coping with unanticipated hardships; we have more evidence that colleges benefit from building in flexibility in response to crises that are certain to happen from time to time in some form. These lessons won't "change everything," but they could form the basis for valuable conversations among all the constituencies on campus.

Socioeconomic and Racial Inequality

The mission of higher education institutions includes improving the society in which they operate—not just improving the lives of the students they educate. All participants in the education enterprise have reason to engage not only in issues of racial and socioeconomic inequities on their own campuses, but also with realities of the larger environment.

Basic facts about the circumstances of different groups of students and their opportunities to enroll and succeed in different types of postsecondary institutions provide critical background.

In 2020, median family income for families with children between the ages of 6 and 17—who might be thinking about how they will finance college—was $81,600. But it ranged from $54,700 for Black families to $121,700 for Asian families. More than a third of Black families with children have incomes below $40,000.

Incomes of Families with Children Ages 6 to 17, 2020

	Median	Share below $40,000
All	$81,600	23%
White	$86,300	21%
Black	$54,700	37%
Asian	$121,700	14%
Hispanic	$61,500	29%

Source: US Census Bureau (2021), "Current Population Survey, Annual Social and Economic Supplement," FINC-03.

Paying for college requires saving, not just paying out of current income. Families with low net worth struggle to send their children to college, even when they do not have low incomes. Wealth is even more unevenly distributed than income. The wealthiest 1 percent of families in the United States hold about 40 percent of all household wealth. The wealthiest 20 percent hold almost 90 percent of the wealth. A quarter of families have less than $10,000 in wealth.[4] Racial inequalities in wealth are stark, with the median wealth of White families between the ages of 35 and 54 almost five times as high as the median for Black families and four times the median for Hispanic families.

Median Family Wealth by Race/Ethnicity and Age, 2019

	Median Wealth (in thousands of dollars), 2019					
	White	Black	Hispanic	Other	White/ Black	White/ Hispanic
Under 35	$25.40	$0.60	$11.20	$13.50	42.3	2.3
35 to 54	$185.00	$40.10	$46.10	$154.50	4.6	4
55 and over	$315.00	$53.80	$115.50	$213.20	5.9	2.7

Source: Bhutta et al., "Disparities in Wealth by Race and Ethnicity."

Compounding differences in financial circumstances, preparing and applying for college, making enrollment choices, and succeeding in earning a degree is more challenging for first-generation students than for those whose parents have the experience to provide guidance. In 2020, when 48 percent of adults 25 or older in the United States had an associate degree or higher and 38 percent had at least a bachelor's degree, only 21 percent of Hispanic adults and 28 percent of Black adults had completed bachelor's degrees.

Educational Attainment of Adults Ages 25 and Older, 2020

	AA or higher	BA or higher
All	48%	38%
White	48%	38%
Black	38%	28%
Asian	67%	61%
Hispanic	30%	21%

Source: US Census Bureau, "Educational Attainment in the United States," Table 1.

Children from different racial and ethnic groups, at different levels of income and wealth, and with parents with different educational backgrounds grow up in vastly different circumstances These differences are associated with how well prepared they are for college, how well they can navigate the enrollment process, and what kinds of external support—financial, academic, and social—they need to succeed in college.

Responding effectively to the challenge of creating a more diverse community is likely to require not only financial trade-offs but also a willingness to respond positively to a broader range of cultural expectations and educational practices. This need is sometimes framed as switching perspective from expecting students to be ready for college to also expecting the college to be ready for the students it enrolls.

CHAPTER ONE

Colleges, College Students, and College Finances

THIS CHAPTER will provide an overview of the variety of colleges and universities in which students in the United States enroll and the degrees they confer, the diversity of the student body, and patterns of revenues and expenses. Too many faculty members, administrators, and trustees think of their own institution as a unique community that must solve its own problems without learning from others. It can be just as problematic when participants in an institution think they should imitate other places without considering relevant differences in circumstances. Understanding where the college or university fits in the larger universe of higher education can help us to know why stories about other institutions may sometimes hold valuable lessons, but at other times might emerge from entirely different circumstances and not provide useful models.

It is easy for many to think of colleges as the places where high school graduates go to mature, decide what they want to do with their lives, and earn the credentials that will open doors for them. But many college students are older adults, and about half of undergraduate college credentials are associate degrees and shorter-term certificates. And graduate students account for a significant share of university operations. Trends in enrollment patterns across

demographic groups provide insight into the role higher education plays in providing opportunities for individual advancement,
as well as in reinforcing and/or diminishing inequality and social
mobility.

Everyone wants to know how expensive college is and why. In addition to reviewing these questions, this chapter will raise questions
about college access and success, highlighting the stratification of
students from different backgrounds into different institutions and
reviewing the success rates of students who enroll in college. One
goal of this discussion is to encourage all campus participants to
reflect on where increasing access and success and reducing socioeconomic and racial stratification in higher education should be on
their agendas.

Higher Education Institutions and Degrees Awarded

In 2019–20, there were 3,982 degree-granting postsecondary institutions in the United States, an increase from 3,192 (26 percent)
40 years earlier. Forty-one percent of these institutions are public—
almost equally divided between two-year and four-year institutions.
Another 39 percent are private nonprofit, and 18 percent (697) are
for-profit. In proportional terms, the biggest changes have been in
the for-profit sector, which grew from 131 institutions in 1979–80 to
1,199 in 2009–10, before dropping to 697 in 2019–20. Public and
private nonprofit institutions are slower to open and slower to close.
Nonetheless, the number of public four-year colleges and universities
rose from 549 in 1979–80 to 614 in 1999–00 and to 772 in 2019–20
(see figure 1.1).

Understanding the variation across states can help to put your
institution into context. Small states such as Alaska, Delaware, and
Rhode Island have fewer than five public institutions; California
has 151 and Texas has 109. The share of public institutions not offering four-year degrees ranges from zero in Alaska, Delaware, and
Nevada to more than three-quarters in five states. There are no private nonprofit four-year institutions in Wyoming, but more than
half of the colleges and universities in seven states are in this sector.
And there is considerable variation within sectors in the extent to
which four-year institutions are heavily focused on research and

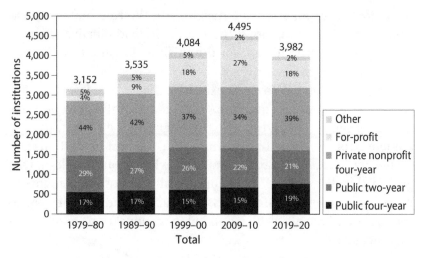

FIGURE 1.1. Postsecondary Institutions by Sector
Source: US Department of Education, *Digest of Education Statistics 2020*, Table 317.10

graduate students or are exclusively educating undergraduate students.

One-fifth of the postsecondary credentials awarded in 2018–19 were graduate degrees, with about four times as many master's degrees as research and professional doctoral degrees combined. Just over half of the undergraduate credentials were bachelor's degrees, with the remainder almost evenly split between certificates and associate degrees (figure 1.2). In other words, the colleges and universities facing challenging decisions about maintaining enrollment and allocating limited resources to instruction, salaries, infrastructure, and other critical aspects of the educational experience don't just have different business models, different sizes, and different student demographics. They have a wide range of educational missions.

Here is one illustration of how this variation matters. Many mid-size institutions, both public and private, have extensive graduate programs. Some of these programs have direct connections to future jobs (like MBAs and law degrees) while others, like master's or PhD programs in history or philosophy, are less directly linked to labor markets. In the last decade, the federal government has made it possible for all graduate students to borrow the entire cost (including living expenses) of their education and at the same time

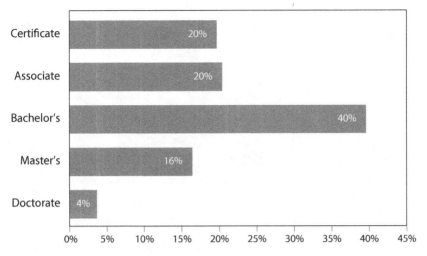

FIGURE 1.2. Degrees and Certificates Awarded by Postsecondary Institutions, 2018–19
Source: US Department of Education, *Digest of Education Statistics 2020*, Table 318.40

has started offering a repayment program that is likely to result in many of these graduate students having a significant fraction of their debt forgiven.

These developments create incentives for universities to expand their graduate programs and for students to enroll in programs even if they have little economic payoff. These facts give universities with substantial graduate enrollments an opportunity for serious campus debate. To what extent should universities promote enrollment in graduate programs with limited career prospects, even when the cost of paying for them is likely to be borne in large part by taxpayers?

College Enrollment

The share of high school graduates who transition immediately to college rose from 45 percent in 1960 to 60 percent in 1990 and then to 69 percent in 2018. And a significant share of the 30 percent who followed other paths have at least tried college by the time they are 30. But, as figure 1.3 shows, the patterns differ markedly across demographic groups. High school graduates from families in the upper quintile of the income distribution are more likely than

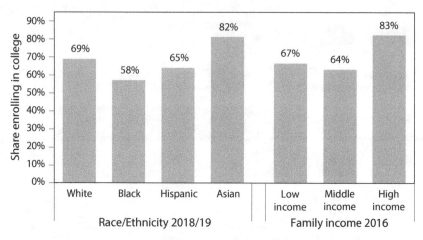

FIGURE 1.3. Share of Recent High School Graduates Enrolling Immediately in College
Note: Family income is divided into lowest 20 percent, middle 60 percent, and highest
20 percent. Latest available data by income are for 2016.
Source: US Department of Education, *Digest of Education Statistics 2020*, Table 302.20;
Digest of Education Statistics 2017, Table 302.30

others to go to college. Larger shares of White and Asian students than of Black and Hispanic students continue their education after high school.

College enrollment does not look the same for all students. In 2019, three quarters of students (but only half of graduate students) attended public institutions; 21 percent were at private nonprofit institutions, with 5 percent in the for-profit sector. Women significantly outnumber men among both undergraduate and graduate students. And about 40 percent at both levels attend part time (see figure 1.4).

Students from different racial and ethnic groups also have different enrollment patterns, as figure 1.5 shows. Most notably, White students comprise a larger share of the student body at private nonprofit institutions than at public institutions, and a much smaller share at for-profit institutions. For-profit institutions have by far the largest share of Black students—32 percent compared with 14 percent overall.[1]

As campuses strive for greater diversity and inclusion, they need to accept the need to invest in creating a culturally responsive environment that will encourage all students to see themselves as full

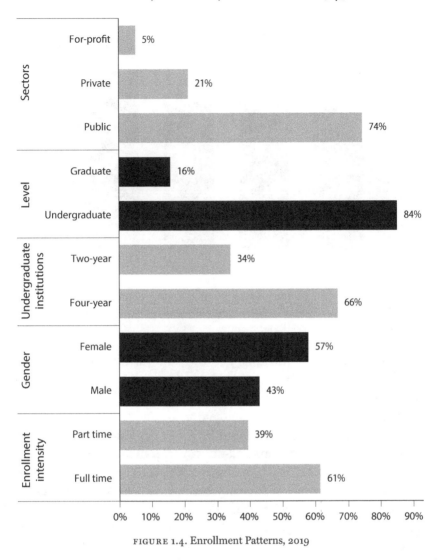

FIGURE 1.4. Enrollment Patterns, 2019

members of the campus community. These efforts involve costs that must be factored into the finances of the institution.

State and Local Funding of Public Higher Education

Total state and local funding for higher education—which included $428 million in COVID relief funds—was higher in 2019–20 than at any other time over the past 40 years. But enrollment in public

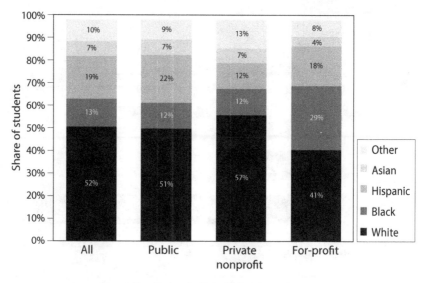

FIGURE 1.5. Enrollment by Race/Ethnicity and Sector, 2019
Source: US Department of Education, *Digest of Education Statistics 2020*, Table 306.50

colleges and universities has grown dramatically over this time period, from 6.9 million full-time equivalent (FTE) students in 1980 to 8.7 million in 1990 and 8.4 million in 2000. Between 2000 and 2010, enrollment grew by 36 percent to 11.4 million, before declining to 10.9 million in 2020. Funding levels per student vary widely across states, ranging from $3,800 in Vermont and $4,750 in New Hampshire to $19,580 in Alaska and $20,020 in Wyoming in 2019–20. Changes in per-student funding between 2009–10 and 2019–20 ranged from declines of over 30 percent in Arizona and Oklahoma to increases of over 40 percent in New Mexico, Oregon, and Wyoming[2] (see figure 1.6).

The enrollment growth coupled with slowing expansion of public funding explains much of the decline in funding per student over the past twenty years. The 2020 funding level of $10,000 per FTE student reflected eight consecutive years of increases, as enrollment declined. But the current funding level is still far below the peak of $11,300 (in 2020 dollars) per student in 2000 and 2001. Public universities have experienced intense pressure on their finances for a number of years now, making campus debate on trade-offs increasingly tense.

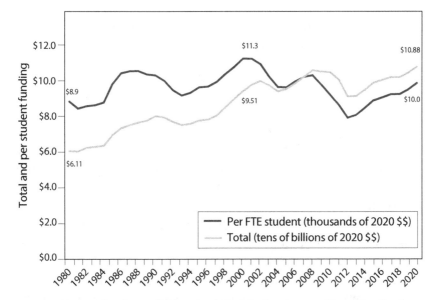

FIGURE 1.6. Total and per Full-Time-Equivalent Student State and Local Funding for Public Higher Education, 1980 to 2020 (in 2020 dollars)
Note: Funding includes federal stimulus funds from 2009 through 2012 and in 2020
Source: State Higher Education Executive Officers (2021), State Higher Education Finance Report FY 2020

Table 1.1. Full-Time Equivalent Enrollment in Public Institutions, 1980–2020

	Millions of FTE students	5-year percentage change
1980	6.9	
1985	7.1	3%
1990	7.8	10%
1995	8.1	4%
2000	8.4	4%
2005	9.9	18%
2010	11.4	15%
2015	11.1	−2%
2020	10.9	−2%

Source: State Higher Education Executive Officers (2021), State Higher Education Finance Report FY 2020.

College Prices: Sticker Prices and
Prices Net of Financial Aid

The published or sticker tuition prices colleges post are not a good indicator of how much students actually pay, because of the prevalence of discounts (or financial aid) institutions provide, as well as supplemental grant aid from the federal government, states, and other sources. But the sticker prices are visible and the source of considerable controversy. Some students do pay these prices, and many others don't understand in advance that they won't have to pay so much.

There is a strong correlation between changes in state and local funding per student and tuition prices at public institutions, as figure 1.7 indicates. Periods of decline in per-student funding correspond to the years with the most rapid increases in tuition and fees, with the largest increases in sticker prices occurring following the recessions of the early 1990s and early 2000s, as well as the Great Recession of 2008–09.

But other factors also contribute to price increases. First, declines in public funding tend to lead to a combination of reduction in expenditures and increases in price. The balance differs over time and among different types of institutions. There is strong evidence suggesting that reductions in expenditures resulting from the failure of state appropriations to keep up with rising enrollments have contributed measurably to increases in time to degree and declines in completion rates, particularly at institutions educating less well-prepared students.[3]

Some institutions have alternative revenue sources. For example, public flagship universities can attract out-of-state and international students—who pay higher tuition than state residents—more easily than broad-access public institutions. In the private nonprofit sector, where state appropriations are not an issue, a small number of colleges and universities hold significant endowment assets, which allow them to cover a significant share of their expenditures from non-tuition sources. Others are almost entirely dependent on tuition revenues and therefore more vulnerable both to enrollment declines and to economic circumstances limiting students' and families' ability to pay.

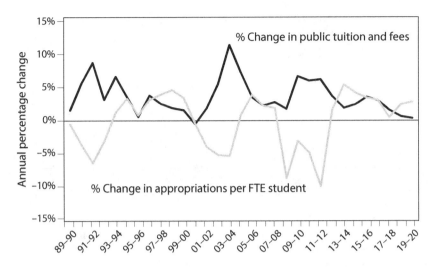

FIGURE 1.7. Annual Percentage Changes in Inflation-Adjusted Per-Student State and Local Funding for Higher Education and in Tuition and Fees at Public Institutions, 1989–90 to 2019–20
Source: The College Board, *Trends in College Pricing 2021*, Figure CP-11A.

In all sectors, tuition increases reflect cyclical economic conditions, but the largest effects are at public four-year colleges and universities (figure 1.8). From 1981–82 through 2000–01, sticker prices at public two-year, public four-year, and private nonprofit institutions rose at about the same rate, doubling (after adjusting for inflation) in about 17 years. But after the 2001 recession, tuition prices at public four-year institutions rose dramatically—by 38 percent from 2000–01 to 2005–06, compared with increases of 15 percent and 17 percent in the private nonprofit four-year and public two-year sectors. Figure 1.8 shows that, despite the fact that concerns about rising tuition have not abated, prices have leveled off, even before the 2021–22 decline associated with the pandemic. Over the five years from 2015–16 to 2020–21, the most rapid increase was 6 percent in the private nonprofit sector.

Of course, students and families feel tuition increases in dollars, not percentages as shown in figure 1.9. And the dollar increases are always largest at private colleges and lowest at community colleges, where tuition is about one-third of the price tag at public four-year institutions.

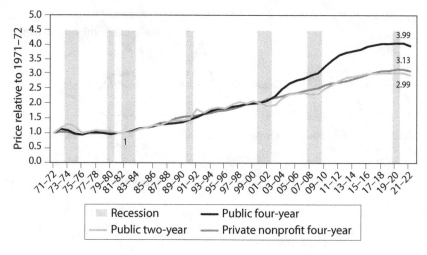

FIGURE 1.8. Increases in Tuition Prices over Time
Note: Shaded areas reflect recessions.
Source: College Board, *Trends in College Pricing 2021*, Table CP-2

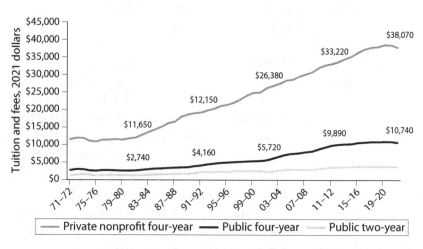

FIGURE 1.9. Dollar Increases in Tuition Prices Over Time
Source: College Board, *Trends in College Pricing 2021*, Table CP-2

College Prices: Net Prices Students Pay

Published prices overstate the amount of tuition students pay because so many students receive grant aid that helps them cover these charges. Some of this aid is out of institutions' control. For example, federal grants, mostly through the Pell grant program, support low- and moderate-income students, primarily those from families with annual incomes below about $60,000 and those responsible for their own support. Some states also focus on need-based aid for those with the most limited resources, but others give out "merit" aid that is based on high school grades and test scores. Changes governments make to their aid policies, for example when the federal government increases the size of Pell grants or a state introduces a merit aid program, can create opportunities and challenges for individual institutions, and these may look different from the perspective of different campus groups. For example, a big increase in Pell could induce an institution to cut back on its own aid commitments, but equally well could provide an opportunity to expand its commitment to enrolling low-income students.

From the institution's perspective, Pell grants and other aid from outside sources are revenues—payments that help cover the cost of enrolling students. But these bills are frequently a lot smaller than the sticker prices suggest. Almost half of undergraduate students attending one institution full time in 2017–18 received grant aid from their institutions averaging about $13,000. At private non-profit four-year institutions, about three-quarters of these students received an average of $22,000 in institutional grant aid[4] (see figure 1.10).

The share of students receiving grant aid declines as incomes rise, but 60 percent of full-time students from families with incomes of $100,000 or higher receive grant aid from at least one source[5] (figure 1.10). Average tuition and fees at public four-year institutions rose by $850 (in 2021 dollars) between 2011–12 and 2021–11; average tuition, fees, room, and board rose by $2,180; but net tuition and fees actually fell by almost $1,000, while net tuition, fees, room, and board rose by $340 after adjusting for inflation. At private four-year institutions, where tuition and fees rose by $4,750 over the decade, tuition and fees net of grant aid fell by $770 because grant aid grew more than enough to cover the increase. Net tuition, fees, room, and board rose by $800.[6]

Family Incomes

Rising tuition prices explain only a part of the stress experienced by students and families facing college expenses. One issue is that tuition is a small share of the expenses most students have

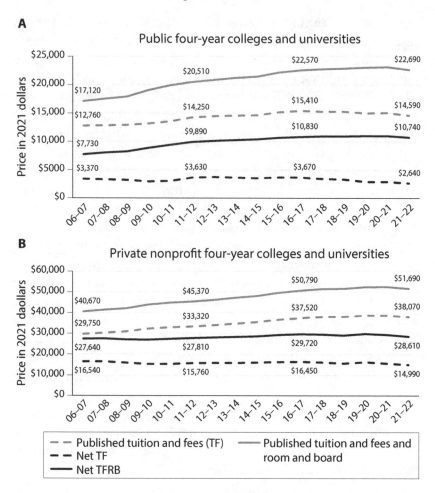

FIGURE 1.10. Net Prices: How Much Students Pay for Tuition
and Fees and Room and Board
Source: College Board (2021), *Trends in College Pricing 2021*, Figures CP-9 and CP-10

to manage. At community colleges, sticker-price tuition and fees account for about 20 percent of official student budgets, which include books and supplies, housing, food, transportation, and other living expenses in addition to tuition and fees. At public four-year institutions, tuition and fees account for about 40 percent of the budget for students living on campus.

The level of income inequality in the United States is now quite high by historical standards and by comparison to other countries

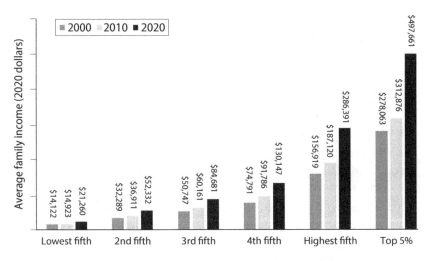

FIGURE 1.11. Mean Family Income by Income Level 2000 to 2020
Source: US Census Bureau (2021), *Annual Social and Economic Supplement*

(see figure 1.11). In 2020, the average income for the top 5 percent of families was $497,661 per year. The average income for the bottom 20 percent of families was just $21,260 per year. Even when high and low incomes grow at the same percentage rate, the gap in purchasing power continues to grow. A 10 percent increase in income for the average top 5 percent family is almost $50,000 compared with $2,126 for the bottom quintile.

The reality is that paying for college is a quite reasonable undertaking for families in the upper quintile of the income distribution, but obviously daunting for those in the middle and below. The reality of this challenge makes the issues facing decision makers on college campuses all the more difficult[7] (see figure 1.11).

Summary

Every college and university is unique in some ways but shares core components of its mission with others. All institutions face decisions about trade-offs in the allocation of resources and decisions about how best to serve students and other constituencies. Understanding where an institution fits in the diverse national higher education system can create context for learning from others while tailoring decisions to particular circumstances.

The public, private nonprofit, and for-profit sectors of higher education all include less-than two-year institutions that grant only short-term certificates, two-year colleges that award primarily associate degrees and certificates, and four-year institutions that may grant only bachelor's degrees or may award a significant number of master's, doctoral, and /or professional degrees. These differences are associated with different financing patterns, different focuses on teaching as compared to research and community service, and a range of other differences in competing priorities.

Some institutions are more vulnerable than others to fluctuations in enrollment. Their student bodies differ by age, academic preparation, race and ethnicity, socioeconomic background—and goals.

But all colleges and universities face challenges with controlling price increases, with helping students navigate the system of financial aid that creates a sizeable difference between sticker prices and the net prices students actually pay, and with operating in an environment characterized by increasing economic inequality and a larger share of potential students facing significant financial challenges.

Many colleges and universities set their own prices and decide for themselves how to distribute their own funds toward financial aid (with the important exception that some states directly set the tuition prices of their public institutions and may have a strong hand in how their resources are deployed for student aid.) But every college or university competes with other institutions, and the competitive environment often exerts strong pressure on campus decisions about pricing and aid. If, for example, a university seeks more revenue by raising its net price, it may find that it instead winds up losing enrollment to lower-priced competitors.

Thus, a broad understanding of the diverse environment in which your institution operates creates important context for developing a framework for decision-making and applying constructive tools and concepts to analyzing the challenges your institution faces.

CHAPTER TWO

Basic Economic Concepts and College Financing

When Dwight Eisenhower was President of Columbia University, he made remarks in which he addressed members of the faculty as "employees of the university." Professor Isidore Rabi (a Nobel prize-winning physicist) interrupted him, saying "Excuse me, sir, but the faculty are not employees of the university. The faculty are the university!"[1]

TO CARRY ON a constructive conversation about college finances and their relationship to the educational mission of the institution, we need to have a common vocabulary. Many terms that crop up in campus debates are laden with connotations unappealing to one constituency or another. For example, faculty who hear trustees or regents discussing the *demand for the product* at their institution are quite likely to fear that those using this terminology are failing to focus on the unique nature of the services faculty provide. Administrators responsible for institutional finance may be frustrated by faculty who argue that attempts to measure their output and increase their productivity suggest a serious misunderstanding of their work. And faculty may despair of trustees or finance officials who think that the worth of a college major can be adequately captured by measuring earnings a year, or three years, after college graduation.

Perhaps familiarity with economic terminology will allow those whose primary responsibility lies in shaping educational opportunities for students to participate more effectively in financial conversations. It may also allow those with responsibility for the bottom line to be clearer about distinguishing between the forces shaping higher education finance and those at work in for-profit markets for goods and services.

The first step in this process is to define economic concepts that are relevant to a wide range of issues but have particular meaning in the context of college and university finance.

Opportunity Cost

Opportunity cost: *The value of the best alternative forgone in making any choice.*

Perhaps the single most important concept all participants in college operating and finance decisions must understand and internalize is that of trade-offs. On some level, we all know that we can't have everything we want and that to get some of the things that are important to us, we must sacrifice other good things. But this reality is too frequently forgotten when we are dealing with the large dollar amounts that appear in institutional budgets and attempting to balance the legitimate interests of a variety of groups.

The **opportunity cost** of a purchase or a decision is the value of the best forgone opportunity. Before you buy a new pair of running shoes, you should think about what else you might choose to do with that money. If you decide to go to the movies, the cost is not just the ticket price, but also the benefit you are giving up by not going to bed early and getting extra sleep or using the time to finish the book you have been reading.

The cost of attending college is not only, and often not mainly, tuition and fees. Students who devote themselves to their studies are giving up the opportunity to participate more fully in the labor market. The opportunity cost of their time—their forgone wages— is part of the full cost of attending college. In contrast, since they would eat and pay rent whether or not they were in college, these are not actual costs of attending college, even though they are expenses students frequently struggle to cover—because they don't have time to work enough for pay to earn a living wage. (Students who could live with their parents if they were not in school but must pay rent to be close enough to campus do in fact incur real additional costs for rent and likely pay more for food than they would if they were not in school.)

Opportunity cost is a useful concept in many campus discussions. We must, for example, decide how frequently to replace campus computers. Most of us agree that up-to-date technology is a good thing. Most of us would rather have a new computer than an older one. We would like the best technology in every classroom to provide the most opportunity for enhanced instruction. But the debate should not be over whether these things are good or not. The question is what we will be giving up in exchange. Are we willing to have lower salary increases to pay for this level of technology? Are we willing to forego the new gymnasium? Are we willing to cut back on student aid and limit access to our institutions? (This last question looks very different at a selective institution that turns away students who want to enroll than it does at a nonselective institution that strives to enroll enough students to fill its classes.)

Active faculty engagement in campus decisions ensures that a broad range of perspectives and interests will be brought to the table and allows more members of the community to feel part of the institution's planning. But this activity takes time and energy that could be devoted to teaching and research or to family responsibilities. This is an opportunity cost that cannot easily be measured in dollars and cents.

The bottom line is that arguments that are simply about why a proposed innovation would be a good thing are incomplete. The debate must include opportunity cost, posing the question of why the benefit from the addition of the proposed program or activity will be greater than the cost of losing something we are now doing or of foregoing an alternative innovation. Sometimes these benefits and costs cannot easily be translated into dollars. Think of the troubling decisions the pandemic imposed in trading off the value of in-person education against the higher risk of infection implied by gathering in the classroom. We do not suggest that this matter should be decided by weighing dollar costs. But that should not stop us from trying to be explicit about weighing what we are getting against what we are giving up.

Total Cost and Net Revenue

Total cost: *The amount spent on producing goods or services over a specified period of time.*

Net revenue: *The amount by which revenues exceed expenses. In for-profit enterprises, net revenues go to the owners. In nonprofit enterprises, net revenues must be saved, so funds are either invested in the institution's mission or saved as financial assets that can be drawn on to make future investments.*

Profit-making firms are interested in maximizing the difference between their revenues and their costs. Despite their primary mission of providing educational opportunities, nonprofit colleges and universities must also pay considerable attention to managing both revenues and costs. Economists have some precise concepts that are useful in understanding many of the decisions colleges and universities face with respect not only to setting tuition and salaries and determining the optimal size of the student body, but also to developing and maintaining academic programs and supporting research.

The concept of **total cost** is simplest. It refers to all of the institution's expenditures over a certain period of time, such as an academic year. The economic concept of cost is different from the accounting concept in that it includes opportunity costs. A firm which is making a 1 percent rate of return on its investment will, for accounting purposes, have positive profits. But from an economic perspective, the opportunity cost of the invested funds—the return they could have generated in the best available alternative use— must be taken into consideration. In economic terms, this firm is probably suffering losses since its revenues do not cover its opportunity costs. Investing these funds elsewhere would likely have generated a higher return.

Similarly, if a college enrolls 50 students to whom it grants tuition waivers, it does not actually give money to these students. But if these 50 students take the place of 50 paying students, then the tuition waivers constitute a very real cost. As discussed in more detail in chapter 7, this idea creates ambiguity in discussions of how much institutional financial aid to offer. If the college could replace a student who will only enroll with financial aid (a discount from the tuition) with a student who would be able and willing to pay the full price, choosing the aided student involves a financial cost to the institution. But if there is no queue of students with a reasonable chance of succeeding at the institution who could pay the full price, enrolling the aided student is not a cost. The choice is between receiving partial tuition and no additional revenue at all.

Some nonprofit organizations rely solely on donations from individuals, foundations, or other philanthropic sources. Others sell things such as cookies or museum store merchandise to fund their missions. Symphony orchestras sell tickets to their performances— and colleges and universities charge tuition. The fact that most colleges and universities—and virtually all of those where shared governance is central—are nonprofit doesn't mean they don't have to worry about increasing revenues and holding costs down. They don't have owners to pay. But to provide quality education, they must cover their costs. And if they want to invest in their operations and improve over time, they have to earn a surplus above what's needed to cover their immediate costs. And they must use those funds efficiently if they want to maintain or raise their quality.

Marginal Costs and Benefits

Marginal cost: *The amount by which producing an additional unit of a good or service increases total costs.*

Marginal revenue: *The amount by which revenue increases when an additional unit is supplied.*

In addition to giving more consideration to trade-offs and opportunity costs, many debates about college investments would benefit from thinking clearly about marginal costs and benefits (including gains and losses we don't measure in dollars and cents), rather than focusing on prioritizing overall expenditure categories. Even if it is obvious that paying the faculty is more important than landscaping, an extra $10,000 spent beautifying the campus could bring a greater benefit than adding that amount to the compensation budget. Students visiting campus respond to its appearance, and it might not take a lot of resources to attract a few more tuition-paying students. In less crass terms, adding a modicum of beauty and grace to the campus may support better learning or a happier environment, or might just attract added enrollment. A small salary bump for a few people might have less impact.

Many decisions are about marginal changes, not about totally eliminating activities or undertaking entirely new endeavors. If you are looking for a new apartment, you may have to choose between one with a bigger living room and another with a better view. Of course, you wouldn't give up either a living space or windows. But you will have to decide which marginal sacrifice will cause you the least pain.

How should the college prioritize upgrading the software it uses for scheduling classes, reducing the copay on employee insurance policies, or replacing classroom furniture? The comparison should be among the changes each of these choices would generate.

The distinction between **marginal cost** and **average cost** can be confusing. For example, the average cost of educating students, or the cost per student, is the total amount spent on education divided by the number of students. If a college spends $100 million a year to educate 5,000 students, the average cost of education is $100 million divided by 5,000, or $20,000.

Does this mean that the college should not accept a student from whom it cannot collect $20,000 of tuition unless it is making a conscious decision to take a loss on the student to provide broader opportunity or diversity in the student body or in some other way to obtain a specific benefit? No. The relevant concept for making this decision is **marginal cost**. Marginal cost is the change in total cost that results from producing one more unit—in this case from enrolling one additional student. The marginal cost of additional students is frequently much lower than the average cost. Once the classrooms and dormitories are built and the faculty hired, an extra student doesn't add much to the cost of operation. There is a limit to this of course. If the college decides to enroll two hundred additional students, it will probably have to hire additional personnel and expand facilities. But for most institutions, the marginal cost of a few extra students is quite low.

The marginal/average contrast explains, for example, why airlines sell seats at low fares if they think they will not otherwise be filled. Once the plane is flying, the marginal cost of additional passengers is very low. If the total cost of flying an airliner with a capacity of 500 passengers is $350,000, the airline will lose money if it doesn't charge an average of at least $700 per person. But it makes sense to let an extra person come on board at the last minute even if he is willing to pay much less than this—just enough to cover any extra fuel cost resulting from the additional weight.

To determine whether the school's financial situation will improve with the enrollment of a student who pays, say, $3,000 in tuition, the relevant question is whether $3,000 covers the marginal cost of educating the student. Does the student add more to revenues than she does to costs? If so, from a purely short-term financial perspective, the student should be enrolled.

And yet the long run matters too. Sometimes a school discovers year after year that it can improve its bottom line by enrolling a few more students than planned. At some point, though, dorms get more crowded, seminars are overenrolled, teachers have too many papers to grade, and educational quality declines. A series of marginal modifications may add up to some big changes.

Demand

Demand: *The amount of a product or service people want to buy at any possible price—backed by both ability and willingness to pay.*

Anyone who has taken an introductory economics class knows that the concepts of demand and supply are fundamental to almost any discussion of economic issues. A basic rule of economics is that the quantity of goods and services people choose to buy depends on prices. When apples go up in price, people may choose to buy fewer

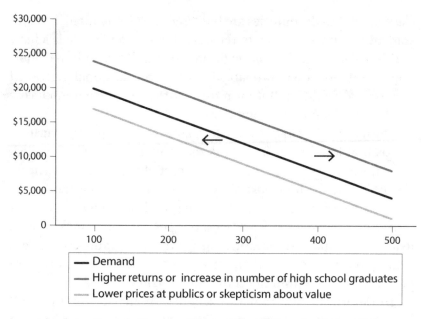

FIGURE 2.1. Example: Downward Sloping Demand Curve for a Private College

apples and more oranges. As the price of apples falls, more people will pay attention to the maxim that an apple a day keeps the doctor away.

It's essential to grasp that "demand" describes a relationship between the amount of a product or service people are willing and able to buy and its price.

There are downward sloping ***demand curves*** for most goods and services, including higher education. The "slope" here refers to a diagram with price on the vertical axis and quantity on the horizontal axis (see figure 2.1). So, as the price falls, the quantity demanded increases. This is not just relevant for apples. As tuition goes up at a particular college, some people decide to go to a cheaper one. And if the price of college generally goes up, some people will decide going to college is not worth it after all.

All other things being equal, more people choose to enroll at a lower price. If the earnings of graduates rise, raising the return, more people will enroll at any given price. The demand curve shifts right. If the price of public colleges goes down, fewer people will enroll in private colleges at any given price. The demand curve shifts left.

The slope of the demand curve reveals how much the quantity demanded changes when the price changes. A steep demand curve reflects small responses to changes in price, while a flatter curve indicates larger increases in the quantity demanded as the price falls.

Determining the position and slope of a demand curve requires taking many factors into account. These include the size of the population, consumers' preferences, income levels, the distribution of income, and the prices of goods and services that might be substitutes or complements (goods that are consumed together with the goods in question). If any of these factors changes, the whole demand curve may shift and its steepness may change.

For example, an increase in the population of recent high school graduates in the Northeast may mean that at any possible price, the number of students interested in attending a private liberal arts college in New York will be higher. If general skepticism about the value of a liberal arts education increases, the opposite will occur—demand will be lower at any given price. Increasing inequality in the distribution of income might have a similar effect.

Overall demand for higher education tends to increase when a general recession hits the economy, largely because the opportunity cost of college falls when employment is harder to find and pays less. People who lose their jobs see their incomes drop, but with more time on their hands, and little money to spend on leisure activities, they may wind up investing their time in education. The pandemic-induced recession in 2020 was an exception to this pattern in part because so many classes moved online and because of fears about the virus.

It's likely that students from lower-income families are more price sensitive than more affluent students. This is not because lower-income families value education less, but because they find it harder and more expensive to finance their own or their children's education. So, while greater inequality pushes down the incomes of lower-income students and reduces their ability to pay for college, more income for the top group won't raise their demand much. The likely effect is a downward shift in demand for liberal arts (and a boost in demand for shorter-term, more vocational sorts of education). Colleges can try to offset this decline in demand by using financial aid to lower the prices for lower-income students.

If private college prices remain constant, but tuition at the state university increases, the demand for private college education is likely to increase. More people will be willing to pay the liberal arts college price, not because they are responding to changes in its price or because their preferences have changed, but because the price of a close substitute—a reasonable alternative—has increased. When complementary goods become more expensive, the demand for a private college education will decline. If, for example, there is a dramatic increase in airfares, fewer students from other parts of the country are likely to enroll.

It is important to note that demand is a function both of people's preferences and of the amount of money they have. In other words, both willingness to pay and ability to pay matter. Standard economic discussions of demand tend to focus on willingness to pay. People are willing to pay higher prices for the first pizza they buy each week, when they crave pizza, than for the tenth, when they are getting bored eating too much of the same thing. In the jargon of economic analysis, the marginal utility of pizza declines as the consumer has more and more of it in a given time period. The amount of satisfaction delivered by the first pizza is greater than the amount of satisfaction delivered by the tenth, and it is this added satisfaction that determines willingness to pay.

However, the demand curve doesn't just measure how much people want something. It measures effective demand, or demand backed up by dollars. A classic example is the comparison of the amount a poor man is willing to pay for milk for his baby to the amount a wealthy man is willing to pay for milk for his cat. Does the wealthy man's willingness to pay a higher price indicate that he cares more about his cat than the poor man cares about his baby? Does he get more satisfaction from the milk? Or is the poor man simply unable to come up with the cash to pay for the milk?

So just because the market is in equilibrium and everyone willing to pay the price is getting the quantity of milk they demand, this does not mean that everyone has what they need, that everyone is happy, or that society should feel comfortable with the outcome. To paraphrase the Nobel economist Amartya Sen, an economy can be both perfectly efficient and perfectly disgusting.

College officials, particularly those in the admissions and financial aid offices, are acutely aware of the distinction between ability to pay and willingness to pay. The need-based financial aid system is designed to ameliorate the problem illustrated by the milk example. The concept of need-based aid rests on the premise that people interested in attending college and able to benefit from the opportunity should have access, regardless of their ability to pay. Need-based financial aid constitutes an attempt to shift the demand curve out by increasing the resources available to pay for college. (Another way of looking at the phenomenon is in terms of net price. Financial aid lowers the effective price, and at lower prices, more people are able to pay.)

But people with sufficient resources to pay for college may be resistant to paying. They feel entitled to scholarship assistance. They are demanding financial aid to keep them from choosing less expensive alternatives. In other words, willingness to pay interacts with ability to pay in determining the demand for college. Many colleges respond to the problem of students they would like to enroll being unwilling to pay by offering non-need-based aid—frequently called "merit" aid. This aid may be based on academic qualifications or other personal characteristics. Many small private nonprofit colleges give discounts of this sort to all their students, effectively lowering their price.

Despite their nonprofit structures, colleges and universities face competitive pressures. Students may choose other institutions because of price, perceived quality, or specific opportunities available. But lowering the price for students may make it more difficult to retain faculty who are offered higher salaries or lower teaching loads elsewhere and staff who find higher-paying jobs in other local industries.

Public universities in many states find their prices and even their financial aid heavily regulated by state government, but they frequently have some discretion in these areas. Flagship universities with strong reputations may be able to attract out-of-state students who generally pay a substantially higher price than in-state students to increase their revenues, although some states limit the number of slots at the state universities that can be awarded to out-of-state students.

Despite the general patterns described here, it is not always true that higher prices will reduce quantity demanded. There are odd patterns for luxury goods because of the "Chivas Regal" effect. As the price goes up, the good or service becomes more appealing to high-income buyers because they assume it is of higher quality—or because of the prestige associated with it. Some colleges hesitate to lower their prices out of concern that they will no longer be perceived as "elite" and will lose students with high ability to pay.

Price Sensitivity

Elasticity of demand: *The change in quantity demanded in response to a change in price. If demand is elastic, quantity demanded changes more than in proportion to the change in price. An increase in price will cause total revenue (price times quantity) to decline, while a decrease in price will increase revenues.*

If demand is inelastic, quantity demanded changes less than in proportion to the change in price. An increase in price will cause total revenue to increase, while a decrease in price will decrease revenues.

Many colleges, aware that demand will be lower if they raise their price, are interested in knowing how much their enrollments are likely to decline if they raise their net tuition and fees—the amount they charge after considering the discounts they provide in the form of institutional grant aid. They would like to bring in more tuition revenue. Maybe they should raise the price. But if they lose a lot of students when they do this, they will end up with less total revenue. Maybe they should lower their price in the hope that this will increase applications and enrollment. But they would need a lot more students, since each student would be paying less than before.

This question relates to the ***elasticity of demand***. If demand is ***elastic***, a small increase in price will lead to a relatively large decline in the quantity demanded. The demand for Bic pens is elastic because people can easily substitute other brands of pens. But the demand for pens as a whole is likely to be less elastic than that for a particular brand of pens. The demand for writing implements including pencils and chalk will be still less elastic. The demand for replacement durable goods like automobiles or dishwashers tends to be relatively elastic because a small percentage increase in price constitutes a large chunk of the average consumer's budget. In addition, consumers can fairly easily decide to keep their old cars for another year or two. But when a new household forms and they need their first car or dishwasher, demand will be less elastic because postponing the purchase is less feasible.

The demand for some products is notably *inelastic*. This means that although there is probably a downward sloping demand curve, the quantity demanded is not very sensitive to changes in price. The demand for insulin is inelastic because it is a necessity for those who use it and there are no good substitutes. The demand for salt is inelastic because even if the price doubles or triples, consumers won't notice it much in their budgets. But the demand for a particular type of salt (for example, sea salt) will be more elastic because consumers can switch to another type that many will judge to be similar.

How sensitive enrollment will be to price changes at an individual institution is quite different from how students respond to price changes at, for example, all public colleges in the state or a large group of private liberal arts colleges. And the question of whether students opt out of college all together because of the price is more significant from society's perspective than whether they switch to another college, but it is not the question facing individual institutions making pricing decisions.

In some states, Pennsylvania for example,[2] individual public campuses are allowed some discretion in setting their tuition rates. A university in such a state may raise its price, creating a gap in tuition with other campuses. Their goal may be to raise revenue, but if demand for that particular campus is elastic, they will lose revenue instead. This is less likely to happen if all public campuses raise their tuition at once. If Smith College resists giving much non-need-based aid while nearby Mt. Holyoke offers students who can afford to pay generous "merit" awards, Smith may lose some students who would otherwise have enrolled. This is not good news for Smith, but campus groups at Mt. Holyoke may have mixed feelings about that policy shift. If there is high elasticity of demand, revenues will go up when the price drops. But the extra students also bring costs. Faculty will face larger classes or have to teach more, students will find more crowding in the gym, and the treasurer will watch expenditures rise, reducing the revenue gain from the move.

For some college students, price is not the deciding factor in choosing where to attend. Students who do not apply for financial aid consistently report that academic reputation and other qualitative characteristics are the primary factors determining college choice. But the story is quite different for students with more limited financial resources. These students have more elastic demand—they are more concerned about changes in tuition levels and price differentials across schools. Financial constraints are very real for students from low-income families and increasingly for those from middle-income families. Their college choice behavior reflects these constraints. Understanding these differences is a critical part of successful institutional pricing and financial aid strategies.

Price Discrimination: Different Prices for Different Students

Price discrimination: *Charging different prices to different customers for the same goods and services even though the cost of supplying those customers is the same.*

Many products are sold under circumstances that require the seller to charge the same price to all consumers. If grocery stores tried to charge chocolate addicts more for candy than they charge dieters, the dieters would soon start buying candy at low prices and selling it to the chocolate addicts.

There are other products whose sellers can charge different prices to different groups of consumers, depending on the consumers' willingness to pay. Airlines charge business passengers more than vacation travelers. Business travelers have inelastic demand and are not likely to cancel their trips because of fare increases. Demand for vacation travel is much more elastic. Airlines manage to charge different prices to these different groups by imposing restrictions on the lower fares that business travelers are frequently unable to meet. (This is one reason, along with security concerns, why you are not allowed to give or sell your airplane ticket to another person.) If producers can price discriminate, charging each consumer the maximum amount he or she is willing to pay, they can reap higher profits than if they charge everyone a price low enough to get the last consumer into the market.

An example of price discrimination in academia is journal prices that are much higher for libraries than for individual subscribers. This price discrimination works only as long as the consumers can be prevented from trading. If individual faculty members were to pass their personal subscriptions on to the library, the pricing system would fall apart.

Colleges and universities price discriminate when they offer financial aid. The net price is different for different students, despite the fact that they are purchasing the same education. Need-based aid allows students with limited financial resources, who could not attend if they were charged the full sticker price, to pay a lower price. Need-based aid price discriminates on the basis of ability to pay. Other forms of student aid may price discriminate on the basis of willingness to pay. Highly qualified students may be less willing to pay for a particular college because they have a choice among several selective institutions. Less qualified students will be more willing to pay—they will have less elastic demand—because they have fewer options.

Equity and Efficiency

Efficiency: *Using resources to produce as much as possible in terms of both quantity and quality at the lowest possible cost.*

Equity: *Treating people fairly in light of differences in their circumstances. Horizontal equity: Treating people in relevantly similar circumstances similarly. Vertical equity: Treating people in different circumstances appropriately differently.*

Engaging in constructive policy analysis requires selecting a set of criteria by which to evaluate alternatives. It is relatively easy to arrive at a consensus that the best policies are those that are both efficient and fair, but arriving at a clear definition of these concepts is not so simple.

Although it is reasonable to debate the importance of efficiency relative to other priorities, it is straightforward to define *efficiency* in terms of using resources as productively as possible. An enterprise or an economy that produces a variety of products is efficient if it can't produce more of one product without producing less of another. There are no free lunches remaining in an efficient economy. An efficient business won't hire an incompetent worker just to save money, and it won't require workers to attend lengthy meetings for no purpose. Efficient colleges will direct their grant dollars to students who won't enroll without them, instead of wasting money by awarding grants to students who would attend anyway—although such a policy could run into equity concerns if, for example, early decision students received less grant aid than similar students who make their enrollment choice after applying to multiple institutions.

And just because a college may reduce its total spending by replacing regular faculty with adjuncts, that won't necessarily make it more efficient. If such replacement reduces educational quality and drives students away, the policy may be wasteful.

All of us have different views about what is fair and what is not. Ranking options in terms of equity almost always requires subjective judgments. But two categories of equity frequently used by economists can help to highlight significant characteristics of alternatives. *Horizontal equity* requires similar treatment of people in similar circumstances. The issue of what constitute "similar" circumstances—or, what constitute differences that are relevant—of course arises. Often there is wide agreement about which differences are relevant. There are some situations (such as being a fashion model for a men's wear brand) where gender may be a relevant job qualification. But exceptional cases aside, people with the same qualifications for a job should have the same chance of being hired, regardless of their gender or the color of their skin or eyes or hair. All students who make the same mistakes on their exams should receive the same grade. Applicants in similar financial circumstances should be defined as having the same level of need that must be met for them to be able to afford to enroll (although "need" might encompass factors beyond income). Faculty members in the same department, at the same rank and at the same level of seniority who have similar levels of performance should be paid the same amount, regardless of their gender.

Vertical equity refers to the appropriately different ways in which people in different circumstances are treated. Athletes who perform better should have a higher chance than others of being chosen for the team. Like the federal income tax system, the financial aid need analysis system expects families with higher incomes to contribute a higher percentage of their incomes for their children's education. The logic is that the sacrifice required in giving up a certain fraction of income is greater for people with less discretionary income. Paying full professors more than associate professors in the same field who have been on the faculty for the same amount of time is vertically equitable. However, no simple rule of thumb is available to determine the amount by which these salaries should differ.

Efficiency and equity considerations are sometimes compatible and at other times may conflict. Providing universal access to high quality early education is both equitable and efficient. It creates broader opportunities at the same time that it increases the productivity of the future workforce and reduces the probability of people being unable to support themselves. But while it may not seem fair that some young people can't drive nice cars just because their parents don't have much money, it's hard to imagine an efficient system that would give everyone whatever car they choose when they get their driver's licenses. But a system that ensured that everyone had adequate means for essential travel might be fair.

Cutting health care benefits to employees who have already retired might be efficient because it would save money without measurably changing anyone's behavior. But for equity reasons, few people would advocate such a move. (Such a move might be efficient in the short run but could sow mistrust that could later backfire on the institution.) It might seem fair to pay all new assistant professors the same salary but, in most situations, this would significantly hamper the institution's ability to attract qualified people for positions in some fields. In this case, efficiency is likely to win out, on the assumption that faculty quality across departments is more important than equal pay. In contrast, it seems both equitable and efficient to use need-based aid to make it possible for lower-income students who could not possibly enroll without this assistance to come to college. It is both equitable and efficient to ensure that faculty and staff have access to medical care so they can be healthy and work effectively.

Criteria of horizontal and vertical equity are not precise enough or widely enough shared to settle most controversies about how a university should decide a hard case. But these concepts provide a framework that can help advance productive on-campus debate on such questions.

Economies of Scale and Scope

Economies of scale: The circumstance in which cost per unit declines as output increases.

Economies of scope: The circumstance in which producing two goods together is cheaper than producing each of them separately.

Average cost per unit may decline as the quantity produced increases because overhead costs can be spread over a larger number of units. Because of these *economies of scale*, the quantity of inputs does not have to double in order to double the quantity of outputs. It is obvious that, for example, a factory that produces one car each day will face higher per-unit costs than a factory making full use of its equipment and producing 100 cars a day.

Similarly, whether a college enrolls 500 students or 10,000 students, they must pay a president, a human resources director, and a chief admissions officer. A small college may have difficulty supporting well-equipped physics laboratories or large athletic facilities. Schools with fewer students spend less on day-to-day operations, but some costs are fixed and do not grow with enrollments—or at least don't grow in proportion to enrollments. Of course, the educational experience also changes as the size of the student body increases. On one hand, the institution can offer a wider variety of courses and other educational experiences. On the other hand, students may be in larger classes and get less personal attention.

Some institutions struggle to attract enough students to keep their costs per student at a reasonable level. Some debate whether to shrink or grow their incoming classes in order to find the right balance among revenues, costs, and quality.

In an economy dominated by giant multinational companies and in an environment where mergers between large companies are commonplace, it is easy to believe that economies of scale are pervasive. However, some production processes require fixed quantities of inputs to generate a unit of output. Technological advances have not reduced the amount of hairdresser time required to produce a good haircut, no matter how many stylists firms employ. Similarly, creating a superior seminar experience may require a ratio of no more than 10 to 15 students to one professor. Providing similar experiences for twice as many students would require twice as many faculty members.

Detecting where economies of scale exist is important. Colleges and universities may save a considerable amount of money by contracting out some activities to firms that specialize in say, food preparation, which can take advantage of economies of scale unattainable to campus-based operations. But it is equally important to recognize those activities where the search for economies of scale may reduce quality and even change the nature of the product, instead of increasing efficiency. Outsourcing important functions like managing dorm life or even, in some cases, instruction, can undermine a campus's sense of common purpose, a key foundation of the idea of shared governance.

Taking advantage of economies of scale is one important motive for campuses to merge. Very small colleges with enrollments of just a few hundred students may find it hard to offer an adequate variety of courses or to provide counseling services. Mergers can help. Short of mergers, cooperation and resource-sharing across institutions can also be productive. On the "back office" side, joint purchasing agreements and shared computing services can be cost savers, as can curricular cooperation on the teaching side. Every cross-campus agreement does, unavoidably, impose some reduction in institutional autonomy, and many will also threaten some workers' employment. These are tough campus issues that need to be faced openly. It is worth mentioning that cooperative agreements can span sectors as well, with cases of public-private cooperation being familiar. There are even interesting cases of cooperation between community college and for-profit campuses.

Economies of scope exist when firms can produce one product more efficiently because they also produce other related products. These advantages could result from the use of the same inputs or production facilities, from joint marketing programs, or from savings from a common management. It is likely cheaper for one farm to produce both milk and cheese than for each of two farms to specialize in one of these products. The processing of crude oil may result in the production of multiple types of fuel.

Most colleges and universities produce more than one output. Teaching and research are most common. The debate about whether research supports or detracts from the teaching mission of the institution is well-known. The argument that any resources devoted to research must be resources taken away from teaching is perhaps the simplest to understand. But the concept of economies of scope may be useful in seeing this issue differently. The knowledge and experience faculty members gain from their research can increase their effectiveness as teachers. The reputation an institution earns through the professional activities of its faculty may have a positive effect on the students who are attracted to campus, increasing the quality of education available. In other words, the two endeavors may complement each other quite effectively.

In many countries it is common to find institutions that specialize in graduate education and research while others focus principally on undergraduate teaching. These places have determined that efficiencies of specialization outweigh economies of scope. In the United States, many institutions of higher education do specialize mainly in teaching undergraduates, but there are very few US research universities that do not include undergraduates. Indeed, institutions like Clark University and Johns Hopkins that originally did not have undergraduates do now. So, the global variation in these practices suggests that matters of history and culture, as well as pure economics, influence the outcomes—a reality that economists should not forget.

Summary: Does Applying Economic Concepts Detract Attention from the Mission of Higher Education?

Furthering the mission of higher education institutions should be the goal of most campus debates, notably those of public and private nonprofit institutions. Understanding economic concepts and viewing campus issues through their lens does not require a greater focus on the bottom line, a lesser emphasis on how decisions affect the quality of the educational experience offered, or a prioritization of efficiency over equity. The tools and concepts of economics do not generally provide decisive answers. But they can provide greater insights into the trade-offs involved in all choices and a more realistic view of the implications of different decisions for the resources available to carry out the college's mission.

Speaking the same language and understanding how others view the problems that require joint decisions can generate constructive dialogue by helping those with different priorities to learn from others' perspectives. Looking at the potential costs and benefits of alternative paths—including pursuing new curricular areas and choosing among policies designed to diminish inequities— need not imply measuring everything in dollars and cents. Rather, comparing the value of available alternatives more explicitly can lead to more balanced decision-making.

CHAPTER THREE

Building Blocks of College Finance

COLLEGE FINANCE differs in a variety of ways from both personal finance and for-profit business finance. For this reason, many faculty and staff members are unfamiliar with the concepts and principles underlying campus financial deliberations, and many trustees and policymakers confound the realities of college finances with those they have experienced in the business world.

Clarifying the terminology and the building blocks of college finance should help all constituencies to be more valuable participants in campus discussions and debates. It's not enough for all the relevant groups to go to meetings. To further their interests, they must be informed participants. More information about the fundamental financial realities of the institution should create an atmosphere more conducive to respectful dialogue and compromise.

A first step is to understand where the institution gets its revenue and where the money goes. It's also important to know something about the basic economic forces affecting higher education and the environment in which it operates.

Public, Private Nonprofit, or For-Profit: What's the Difference?

As noted in chapter 1, there are 4,000 degree-granting postsecondary institutions in the United States. About 40 percent are public, a similar number are private nonprofit, and almost 20 percent are for-profit. Public institutions tend to be the largest, averaging about 9,000 students (including both undergraduate and graduate students); about three-quarters of students are enrolled in this sector. Private nonprofit colleges and universities, which enroll an average of about 2,500 students, account for about 20 percent of enrollments. And the for-profit sector, which shrank to about half its size between 2012 and 2019, enrolls only about 5 percent of students.

Every state has at least one public higher education institution. Some states rely primarily on four-year institutions that offer bachelor's degrees and usually at least some graduate degrees. In other states, many public sector students attend public two-year colleges (community colleges), which offer primarily associate degrees and short-term certificates. Founded by the states and operated by state governments, public colleges and universities get a significant share of their funding as direct appropriations from state, and sometimes local, governments. The share of total revenues coming from state and local governments has declined over time. But even when that share is small, the state maintains control over many aspects of its public institutions' operations, sometimes including tuition levels.

Private nonprofit colleges and universities get very little funding from state governments, although students at these institutions are generally eligible for state grant aid. Instead, they rely on tuition and fee revenues; donations from alumni, foundations, and other private entities; and if they are fortunate enough, income from the endowment assets they have accumulated over time. No one owns a private nonprofit. No one is allowed to take profits out of the enterprise. Instead, any excess revenues above expenses are either invested in the educational mission or saved for future investments in that mission. Boards of trustees have fiduciary responsibility, overseeing the college's financial operations and generally holding ultimate authority over many decisions.

In contrast, for-profit institutions are either owned by one or more individuals or companies or are publicly held and traded on the stock market. These institutions are designed to generate profits for their owners through the provision of educational services. Their revenue comes primarily from tuition and fees, a significant share of which is covered by the federal and state financial aid the students receive.

Revenues

One of the hurdles to engaging the college community in a reasoned discussion of the intersection of finances and institutional mission is that it is easier to focus on the expenditures educational institutions make in the process of accomplishing their goals than on the revenues required to support these expenditures or on the difficulty of balancing the two. When we think of profit-making businesses, we think of their essence as making money—generating net revenues. Clothing stores and automobile makers and banks provide useful goods and services. But they provide these services because they can make a profit by doing so, not because their primary focus is the well-being or improved living standards of their customers.

Public and private nonprofit colleges and universities, on the other hand, exist because of the service they provide—not merely because of the money they can make providing that service. The tax advantages these institutions receive depend on a judgment by the IRS that they serve a charitable purpose. For most institutions, the central purpose is to educate students well, aiming to help them have more successful careers and be more effective in contributing to their communities. For the 200 or so universities that are major research centers, revenue includes substantial support for the research that is a critical part of their mission, much of it funded by government agencies.

Most college faculty and administrators could have pursued more lucrative careers, but they have chosen not to put money at the top of their priority list. Moreover, their function at work is not

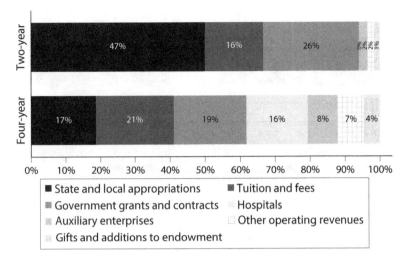

FIGURE 3.1. Sources of Revenue for Public Colleges and Universities, 2018–19
Source: US Department of Education, *Digest of Education Statistics* 2020, Table 333.10

to maximize the institution's revenues or minimize its costs. Of course, those responsible for an institution's finances have a different focus from those hired to teach, but everyone agrees that the purpose of financial strength is to be able to provide valuable educational opportunities and socially useful research—not the other way around. But without adequate revenues, colleges and universities cannot possibly succeed in their mission.

Focusing on generating net revenue may feel to some like a violation of the fundamental, loftier, educational mission. For those whose role within the institution is primarily to ensure financial stability, the core mission may sometimes fade into the background.

State funding for public colleges and universities has not kept up with increases in enrollment. As indicated in figure 3.1, public two-year institutions get almost half their revenues from state and local appropriations, but at public four-year institutions, this share was only 17 percent in 2018–19. The role of this funding source varies considerably across states, ranging from about 40 percent for all public institutions in Alaska and Wyoming to less than 15 percent in seven states.

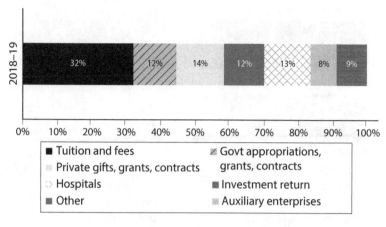

FIGURE 3.2. Sources of Revenue for Private Nonprofit Four-Year
Colleges and Universities, 2018–19
Source: US Department of Education, *Digest of Education
Statistics 2020*, Table 333.40

Tuition and fees made up an average of 21 percent of total revenues for public four-year colleges and universities and 16 percent
for public two-year colleges in 2018–19. The share of revenues from
tuition and fees at public institutions ranges from 8 percent in New
Mexico and 12 percent in Utah to 37 percent in Delaware and
New Hampshire and 45 percent in Vermont.

Revenue sources are quite different at private nonprofit four-year
institutions. A higher share comes from net tuition and fees—about
one-third in 2018–19 (up from one-quarter in 1999–00). Private
institutions also get more of their revenues from private gifts and
contracts—14 percent in 2018–19 and ranging from 11 percent to
16 percent over the preceding decade—than public institutions do.
Figure 3.2 shows 12 percent of revenues coming from investment
returns, but it is important to understand the volatility of this source
of revenue. As shown in figure 3.3, in 2008–09, investment losses were
almost equal to total revenues from all other sources. In 2010–11 and
2013–14, investment gains made up about a quarter of total revenues.

Private for-profit colleges get more than 90 percent of their revenue from tuition and fees. At about 80 percent of these institutions,
more than half of those tuition revenues come from federal grants
and loans to students.

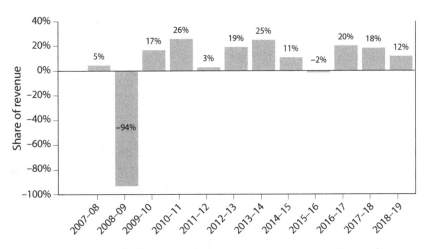

FIGURE 3.3. Share of Revenue from Investment Returns, Private Nonprofit
Four-Year Colleges and Universities, 2007–08 to 2018–19
Source: US Department of Education, *Digest of Education Statistics 2020*, Table 333.40

Tuition Revenues: Gross versus Net

One significant ambiguity involved in measuring institutional revenues has to do with the distinction between gross tuition revenues and net tuition revenues. Gross tuition revenue is calculated by multiplying the number of matriculating students by the tuition charge. This is the standard way of thinking about this budget item.

However, many students do not pay the full stated tuition—the sticker price. Rather, the college gives them a scholarship or financial aid grant. Essentially, they are receiving a price discount.

Suppose the sticker price is $18,000. A student is awarded an institutional grant of $5,000 because of her family's financial circumstances or because of her academic or athletic achievements. In this case, the institution collects $13,000 of revenue. This is the price being charged to this particular student. Counting the entire $18,000 as revenue and $5,000 as an expenditure is basically the same as a car dealer's counting the sticker price of $30,000 as revenue and considering your $6,000 discount an expenditure when you have bargained him down and ended up paying only $24,000 for your car.

Net tuition revenue refers to the amount of tuition revenue the college actually receives. It is the sum of the prices (net of institutional grant aid) paid by each student, sometimes with support from federal or state governments, private scholarships, or other sources. Whether some of the money is borrowed or not does not matter to the calculation of how much revenue comes in.

Net tuition revenue can also be calculated by subtracting institutional grant awards from gross tuition revenue. The bottom line is the same, but the implications are different. If gross revenue is the focus, there is a sense that the dollars spent could have been devoted to financial aid or to computers or to faculty salaries. There is a decision to be made about expenditure priorities. On the other hand, if net revenues are the focus, the choices are more limited. The $13,000 student would probably not have enrolled if the price were $18,000, so deciding how to spend the extra $5,000 is unrealistic. For a small number of institutions, it would be possible to attract a full class of students willing to pay the sticker price with no discounts. But for most colleges and universities, net revenue is a more reasonable starting point for discussions of expenditure priorities.

Net undergraduate tuition revenue is a major factor in the finances of most institutions, and clear thinking about it is important to campus discussion of the fiscal choices the institution faces. At research-intensive universities, graduate education and sponsored research may dwarf the revenue contribution from undergraduates. Morty Schapiro, president of Northwestern University, told us that net undergraduate tuition is only about 8 percent of total revenue there.

The Discount Rate and Financial Aid

The difference between gross and net tuition revenues is an indicator of how much the institution is discounting its price for students—either because the students cannot afford the full price or because the college is using this strategy to convince them to choose this school rather than a different one. Many institutions, particularly private nonprofit institutions, set a target for the discount rate. For a given tuition price, a higher discount rate means lower net tuition revenues. The discount rate is measured as the total institutional grant aid awarded as a percentage of gross tuition revenue—the amount that would be collected if there were no discounts.

It's easy to be misled when thinking about the discount rate as a number to manage. At many private institutions nearly all the students get a tuition discount; almost nobody pays the full sticker price. Consider the extreme case where every student gets a discount of $2,000 or more. The college could decide to cut the sticker price by $2,000 but provide everybody with the same net price as before. If you had a $3,000 scholarship last year, now your tuition would be $2,000 less, but your scholarship would be cut to $1,000. Everybody's economic situation would be unchanged. The discount rate would be substantially lower, but net tuition revenues for the college—which are the true measure of their resources—would be unchanged. The test of whether an institution's financial health is improving is whether net tuition revenue is going up, rather than whether the discount rate is falling.

Some institutions have a clear target either for the discount rate or for net tuition revenue. But some relatively affluent colleges admit students without regard to their need for aid, guaranteeing that every admitted student will have their full financial need met through a combination of governmental and institutional aid. And public institutions in some states have little discretion over how they set prices or award their aid. In both these kinds of cases, the net tuition or the discount rate is not a variable that is actively managed—it is just a number that emerges from the process.

According to the National Association of College and University Business Officers, in 2020–21, private nonprofit colleges and universities reported an average discount rate of 48 percent for all undergraduate students.[1] This means that for every $100 of tuition charged, institutions gave $48 back to students in the form of institutional aid. If they raise tuition by $100, they increase their net revenues by only about half that much. At many institutions, especially those experiencing enrollment declines, this leads to declining net tuition revenues. This is a problem, regardless of where the discount rate lands.

In 2018–19, private nonprofit four-year institutions awarded an average of $18,210 in institutional grants to their first-time full-time

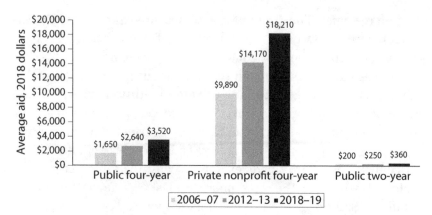

FIGURE 3.4. Average Institutional Grant Aid in 2018 Dollars, First-Time Full-Time
Undergraduate Students, 2006–07 to 2018–19
Source: The College Board, *Trends in Student Aid 2021*, figure SA-19A

students (including both recipients and non-recipients)—$6,800 more than a decade earlier and an increase of 60 percent after adjusting for inflation. Average grant aid per student almost doubled at public four-year colleges and universities, to $3,520. Public two-year colleges give much less of their own aid, but grants also increased significantly at these institutions (figure 3.4).

Expenditures

On the expenditure side, instruction is only a part of the activity the college or university must fund.

The standard accounting system (Governmental Accounting Standards Board or GASB for most public institutions; Financial Accounting Standards Board or FASB for most privates) breaks expenditures down into functions. Key categories include:

Instruction: This most basic category aims to include all expenses for instruction, including research that is not separately budgeted. This is where faculty salaries appear.

Between 2009–10 and 2018–19, the share of total expenditure at public four-year institutions devoted to instruction fell from 29.4 percent to 26.6 percent. At public two-year colleges, the decline was from 42.2 percent to 40.4 percent. But in 2018–19, public four-year institutions spent almost twice as much per student on instruction as public two-year colleges—$12,748 versus $6,937.[2]

The share of expenditures devoted to instruction also fell at private nonprofit four-year colleges and universities, from 32.8 percent in 2009–10 to 30.2 percent in 2018–19, when these institutions spent an average of $19,308 per full-time-equivalent student on instruction.

Academic support: This category includes support services that are an integral part of the primary mission of instruction, research, and public service; it includes libraries, museums, computing support, academic administration, curriculum development, etc. These expenditures are considerably higher at four-year than at two-year institutions.

Student services: Expenditures for recruitment and admission. Registrar, student life, co-curricular, and residential life expenses fall into this category.

Institutional support: This covers day-to-day operational support. It includes general administrative services, legal and fiscal operations, personnel and records, campus security, and some information technology expenses.

Other: Institutional budgets also include separate categories for scholarships and fellowships, for research, and for public service.

The breakdown of expenditures across these categories differs considerably across types of institutions. For example, public two-year colleges spend more on student services relative to instruction than public four-year institutions do. Average per-student expenditures on student services have grown particularly rapidly at private nonprofit four-year colleges and universities. Research and public service comprise a significant share of expenditures at four-year institutions, particularly in the public sector, but not at two-year institutions.

Colleges and universities are labor-intensive operations, both in terms of faculty and support staff. About 60 percent of all college and university spending is accounted for by spending on personnel, according to one recent estimate.[3]

Tuition and Fees, Student Budgets, and Net Price

Much of the public distrust of higher education relates to rising tuition prices. College prices almost always go up faster than other prices in the economy, as measured by the Consumer Price Index (CPI). But it's not true that prices have suddenly started rising rapidly. Even before the impact of the pandemic on prices for 2020–21, recent increases were moderate by historical standards.

In all the major sectors, the average tuition price rose more slowly (after adjusting for inflation) between 2010–11 and 2020–21 than in either of the two preceding decades. Still, the cumulative effect of all these increases is that at private nonprofit four-year colleges and public two-year institutions, average sticker price tuition and fee prices are about twice as high in inflation adjusted dollars as they were 30 years ago. At public four-year institutions they are almost three times as high (figure 3.5).

Looking at the pattern in percentage terms makes the public four-year sector look worse (although prices rose fastest in the private nonprofit sector between 2010–11 and 2020–21). But looking at the dollar amounts changes that story. As figure 1.9 illustrates, in 2020–21, the average sticker tuition and fee price at private nonprofit four-year colleges and universities was $37,650, more than three and a half times the $10,560 average at public four-year institutions. In 1990–91 it was almost five times as high.

But these prices don't reflect either the amount of tuition and fee revenue colleges are collecting, or the amount students are paying. As discussed above, net tuition revenues are lowered by discounting (institutional grant aid). Because discount rates rise over time, the average amount institutions charge (net price) has risen more slowly than these changes in sticker prices suggest (as figure 1.10 illustrates).

Because students also get assistance from federal and state grant aid, employers, and other private sources, the amount they pay differs even more from the sticker prices. From the institution's perspective, net tuition revenues include everything the students pay after institutional aid (discounts), whether they pay it out of their own pockets or with help from federal, state, or private grants and scholarships. But from the student's perspective,

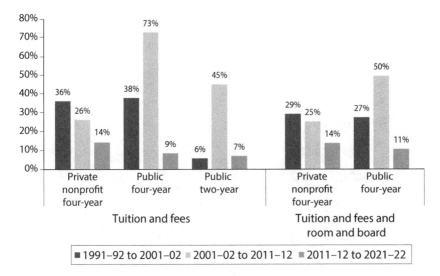

FIGURE 3.5. Ten-Year Percentage Changes in Inflation-Adjusted Published
Prices by Decade, 1990–91 to 2020–21
Source: College Board (2021). *Trends in College Pricing 2021*, Figure CP-4

the net tuition price is what they pay after subtracting grant aid
from all sources. Another way to put this point is to note that the
net tuition institutions receive is larger than the net tuition students
pay. In campus discussion of aid issues, it can help considerably
to be as clear as possible about how a concept like "net tuition" is
being used.

Students' budgets, frequently called "cost of attendance," include
a range of expenses over which institutions have no control. Colleges where students do not live on campus cannot determine housing and food costs. These expenses, plus transportation, books and
supplies, and other living expenses account for about 80 percent
of the budgets (before student aid) of community college students
and an average of 60 percent for in-state public four-year college
students.

As figure 3.6 shows, students from higher-income households
pay more than those from lower-income households. This pattern
is the result of the larger amounts of grant aid available to students
with the most limited financial resources. Moreover, students from
higher-income backgrounds are more likely than others to attend
higher-price institutions, even within sectors.

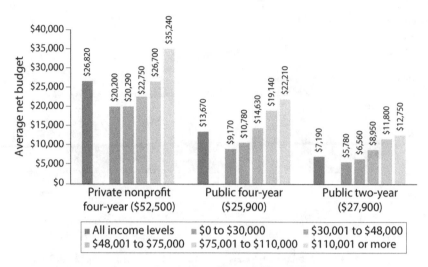

FIGURE 3.6. Average Net Budget for First-Time Full-Time Students
Receiving Grant Aid, 2018–19
Note: Net price is the total budget, including books and supplies and living
expenses in addition to tuition and fees, minus grant aid from federal, state,
and local governments and institutions. Calculations include students
who received federal loans or work-study, but no grant aid.
Source: US Department of Education, *Digest of Education
Statistics 2020*, Table 331.30.

Productivity and Price Increases

Economic productivity is a measure of how much value a worker
provides to the enterprise through an hour of labor. This concept
figures into college issues in at least two ways: the increases in
productivity college education generates among students and the
attempts to measure the value of the output produced by instructors and other college personnel.

The first question is about the creation of "human capital"—the
increase in knowledge and skills resulting from education. There
is considerable evidence that productivity is highly correlated with
level of education and that the US policy of investing more heavily
in education than most other countries is a major factor (along
with investments in science and abundant natural resources) in
explaining the country's strong record of economic growth. This is
an arena for challenging campus discussion: Where should human
capital formation figure into defining a college's mission? What

about other goals of college education like improved citizenship or healthier personal relationships? Should colleges expand departments that offer the best employment prospects for their graduates and shrink (or kill) departments that aren't tightly linked to particular jobs? (We have included a box later in this chapter that offers some perspective on these issues.)

But the second aspect of productivity also deserves attention. How productive are the campus's own workers? Is there a reasonable way to measure productivity for instructors that doesn't just demand that they teach more students? Should their productivity be expected to grow over time? In the economy at large, productivity tends to increase over time, largely because of technological progress and an increasingly educated workforce. Between 2007 and 2020, output per work hour increased at an average rate of 1.5 percent per year in the non-farm business sector—a low rate by historical standards.[4] This increase in productivity allows wages to increase without putting upward pressure on product prices.

Productivity is measured most easily in industries where the output can be quantified without difficulty. Food products and many types of manufactured goods are examples. Defining and measuring productivity in higher education is not so simple. The number of students receiving course credit or degrees can be counted, but few people would argue that these numbers alone are a reasonable measure of institutional output. The quality of educational services and the specific benefits accruing to individual students are the core of the institutional mission but are impossible to quantify or even describe precisely. The value of research produced may be even more challenging to measure.

In fact, one reason why people worry about relying on for-profit suppliers in higher education is the great difficulty in assessing the quality of the services provided. In the absence of good measuring tools, our confidence in higher education has to be based partly on trusting that government and nonprofit providers are aiming to provide the best service they can. Other areas of the economy where nonprofit supply is important include community service, medical services, and psychological counseling, where the quality of services is also hard to measure.

Nonetheless, the goals of higher education certainly constitute a form of output and, as in many other service industries, productivity increases are harder to come by than in manufacturing. To allow compensation to increase without putting upward pressure on tuition, faculty would have to teach more students. Large universities, especially those with graduate students who can work as section leaders, can take advantage of large introductory classes. This strategy runs into limits, though, since it is hard both to achieve scale in more advanced courses and to provide high quality instruction at large scale in such courses. This means that the price of education is likely to rise more rapidly than the prices of many other products—and more rapidly than the CPI. Similar problems occur in other industries in which service providers must be physically present with clients or customers, with the personal relationship placing limits on the scale at which the service can be performed and on the possibilities for cutting costs. Live theater, salon services, and personal training are examples. Hospitals, like universities, are places where substantial amounts of personal attention are needed, and where cost pressures persist.

The tension between salary increases that allow faculty and staff to maintain their relative position in society and rapidly rising tuition levels has been and will continue to be a problem for policymakers in higher education, especially if the salaries of highly educated workers in fields like technology and investment banking continue to rise rapidly. Because it is so difficult to increase productivity for faculty in a way that generates more revenue for their work—unless students pay more tuition—and because compensation is such a large share of the expenditures of colleges and universities, upward pressure on prices is likely to continue.

Increased use of technology for instruction may help to reduce costs. It remains to be seen what the lasting effects of the shift to online learning during the coronavirus pandemic will be. But to date, high quality online learning has not been a cost saver, and personal interaction remains critical, particularly for less academically well-prepared students.[5]

The Challenge of Measuring Productivity: The False Dichotomy of
General Education versus Occupational Preparation

Is the main purpose of higher education to prepare students for a well-paid job, or is it to equip students to lead a rich and satisfying life that includes active citizenship and rewarding participation in artistic and cultural endeavors?

Many institutions are considering—or are already in the process of—transitioning toward preparation for specific occupations in an effort to raise revenues by attracting more students—particularly older students. Many faculty members see such a move as threatening the educational mission. The educational mission of most institutions is broader and deeper than immediate preparation for the labor market. A real challenge facing many higher education institutions is how to ensure that no matter what they study, students are equipped to step into jobs that will allow them to support themselves. And that, no matter how focused they are on specific careers, they develop the perspective and capabilities to be good citizens and to adapt to the unforeseen changes they will face.

Of course, higher education is more than one thing. Many community college programs, as well as much of graduate education, aim primarily at preparation for particular occupations like medical technology, welding, or cosmetology—or law, medicine, or college teaching. The typical bachelor's level student has a major that, whether it has a clear occupational focus or not, involves some form of general education that aims at broadening knowledge and skills, regardless of students' career choices. Interestingly, most BA graduates, even if their major had a clear occupational "hook" like business or engineering, do not wind up in the occupation for which they were trained.[6]

The reality is that, in an economy that is likely to continue to undergo rapid technical change, landing a good job right out of college is very far from ensuring a rewarding career. Comparing career trajectories of people who do and don't have BAs, economists have learned that the big payoffs to college education don't fully kick in until eight or ten years after college, by which time many workers will have moved on from whatever type of work they started in.[7]

Labor market studies document that the skills and talents that have lasting value in the marketplace are those like critical thinking, effective oral and written communication skills, empathy and respect for others, and developed capacities for problem recognition (for example, if we are to succeed, we are going to have to figure out how to do X) as well as problem solving.[8] Career success depends on being able to do well the job you have now, and, even more, on being able to move on successfully to the next job as conditions change. Resourcefulness and the ability to "learn how to learn" are essentials.

These are the kinds of broad skills and capacities that general education requirements and a liberal arts approach to instruction tend to aim at, and that a narrowly job-specific training is less likely to provide.

Thus, a campus dispute between "liberal or general" education and "vocational" education is a false choice. Trade-offs between the time a student spends on general education and on more intense focus on her major are unavoidable, but it's key to recognize that these two dimensions of education are best seen as complementary.

Simple measures of productivity based only on number of degrees granted or on the earnings of graduates shortly after they complete their studies cannot capture this complexity. Nonetheless, it is impossible to monitor the effective use of campus resources without some measures of productivity.

CHAPTER FOUR

Is a College a Business?

The provost was having trouble sleeping. Difficult moments from the day's Board of Trustees meeting kept flashing through his mind. A senior member of the Board had exploded when he heard that the faculty had recommended tenure for a member of the Archaeology Department. Earlier in the day, they had seen figures on enrollments, and this department had the lowest ratio of enrollments to faculty. It had more classes with fewer than 10 students than any other department on campus. And now they wanted to promise lifetime employment to a young teacher/scholar in the field?

The faculty chair of the appointments committee, a professor in the Department of Foreign Languages, could not contain his outrage at the trustee's outburst. The college's Archaeology Department was widely recognized as one of the best in the country. The professor in question was a star—a beloved teacher and a widely published scholar. Denying her tenure would be a violation of the standards for awarding tenure. And it would harm the college's reputation, reducing its appeal to students over the long run. Moreover, wasn't the decision to offer a tenure-track position to that candidate six years ago an implied promise to award her tenure if she met the standard?

The provost saw both sides of the issue. He believed that trustees should interfere in tenure decisions only in the rarest circumstances. But that didn't stop the nagging doubts about making personnel decisions without considering their long-run financial implications.

ANYONE WHO RUNS a for-profit business knows that if costs exceed revenues for long, the business will have to shut down unless someone is willing to pour a lot of money into it. The goal of maximizing profits may not perfectly describe every business venture, but inadequate attention to the bottom line is a recipe for failure.

College faculty and administrators tend to have very different pictures of the way their institutions work. Except for the relatively small share (in terms of enrollments) of institutions that are for-profit, colleges and universities were not founded to make anyone rich. Their mission is to educate students and to expand knowledge. Sacrificing this mission in the interest of increasing revenues or reducing costs violates the sense of purpose shared by many faculty members, staff, and administrators.

When board members with fiduciary responsibilities look to the business sector for models of organization and management, the potential for clashes with campus values and culture is great.

But does this mean that academic institutions have nothing to learn from the business world? Does it mean that worrying about the financial strength of the institution, thinking about demand for the education offered, or adjusting offerings in response to a changing economic environment is contrary to the mission?

Of course not. Colleges and universities compete for students and for faculty and staff. It is expensive to provide education, and someone must pay for it. Students pay tuition and fees, frequently with the help of financial aid from various sources. State and local governments send money to public colleges and universities to fund their operations. Alumni and other philanthropic sources donate money. Without these revenues, the faculty will not be paid. The students will not have up-to-date technology. The dorms and classrooms will fall into disrepair. And of course, colleges and universities don't want to maintain the status quo; they want to improve over time. You can only invest in the future if your revenues exceed your costs.

As we have noted earlier, the decision-making process on many college campuses reflects a model of shared governance, with trustees, administrators, and members of the faculty sharing responsibility and providing input. Trustees from the business world are sometimes dismayed by the amount of consultation and time required to make decisions. The priorities of nonprofit higher education institutions differ dramatically from those of most businesses.

Still, it is not possible to draw a red line between financial strength and educational mission. Much of the logic behind decisions in the business world applies to decisions on campus— even if the fundamental goals are different.

Think back to the concepts introduced in chapter 2.

Opportunity cost: There are always trade-offs, and it is often difficult for advocates of specific valuable projects to fully weigh those trade-offs. It would be better if we had more athletic facilities. State-of-the art technology would improve the classroom experience. Smaller classes are more satisfying than larger ones. Higher salaries will attract better faculty. But we can't do all the desirable things because we have limited resources. There are trade-offs. The opportunity cost of the latest technology all over campus may be that faculty salaries will rise more slowly. The need to face up to such trade-offs is core to decision-making in both businesses and colleges.

Marginal cost: How much will it add to the institution's budget to hire an additional counselor for students with learning disabilities? The debate should not be over whether adequately serving these students is important. What added costs might there be over and above the individual's compensation? Will this department need more office space? Will the added services increase the number of students taking advantage of these services and the amount of attention they expect? Will the added services improve students' academic success, reducing the time it takes them to graduate? In all cases, the question is about the *change*, not about the overall costs and benefits of these services.

If we can get past the language barrier and emotional reactions to terminology that sounds like it is about dollars and cents and not about education, we may be able to make decisions that strengthen the capacity of the institution to serve students well for years to come.

The language of business firms—customers, demand, product, service—seems discordant on a college campus. But using such language need not denigrate the educational and intellectual mission. It is impossible to protect the academy entirely from market forces, and like any other enterprise, higher education institutions face very real resource constraints. Perhaps demystifying some of the market terminology while taking a close look at ways in which colleges differ from other enterprises can facilitate a dialogue on the subject.

A Distinctive Enterprise

A standard type of firm that basic economic models were designed to understand is an enterprise that sells a product or service to customers to make profits. Owners and managers make decisions about how the firm should operate. Other employees are paid to carry out management's decisions. To make profits, the firm must produce offerings that satisfy customers. Failure to meet customer demands as well as other firms do will result in the firm's failure. Firms want to sell their wares at the highest possible price to as many buyers as possible.

Most colleges and universities are not seeking profit and are operating to provide a service. There are no owners, and many of the employees—particularly the faculty—participate actively in management decisions.

Several other characteristics of higher education markedly differentiate it from many other markets. One is the prevalence of subsidies of various types. Despite the increasing prevalence of student loans, most students benefit from some combination of parental contributions, government subsidies, and institutional aid. Institutions with large endowments or generous donors can cover a significant share of the total cost even for students who pay full tuition. Willingness to pay is not merely a matter of the individual student's attitude toward education. State legislators, federal policy makers, donors, and—in the case of traditional-age students—parents, must also be willing to pay. This means that many students who themselves would not be willing to pay the full price will attend—clearly a necessity for the viability of many institutions in the current market.

Students as Customers

Perhaps most grating to the academic ear is the use of the word *customers* to represent students. The simple transaction of a customer exchanging money for a clearly defined good or service is a poor representation of the relationship between a student and her college. The college provides an environment in which a student can work to become educated. The fact that students are paying faculty to teach them is generally far below the surface in their interactions. Rather, they are engaged in a cooperative enterprise with a shared goal.

Other professionals who supply personal services that depend heavily on trust are similarly aversive to language implying a purely commercial relationship—doctors have patients, lawyers have clients, clerics have parishioners.

The idea that colleges must convince students to buy what they have to offer is more likely to resonate with admissions officers. In the admissions office, ensuring that the number of students who sign up meets the goals embodied in the financial model—and that those students have a reasonable chance of succeeding and continuing their enrollment—is front and center. In contrast, instructors have something of a captive audience. They are focused on working with students in the educational process. These students have already chosen to be there. They may leave the institution, but it's unlikely they are weighing that decision each time they go to class.

Nonetheless, in some respects, college students are customers, although they differ from most customers. Aside from having purchased a service that they use over an extended period of time, students cannot benefit from the education they are purchasing unless they bring considerable effort and ability to the task. In this respect, enrolling in college is like joining a gym. And students constitute a major input into the process of producing education since the quality of a student's education is affected by the other students on campus. Considerable evidence points to the importance of "peer effects," through which students benefit from attending college with others who are dedicated and well-prepared students. The quality of your television, in contrast, is unaffected by the character of the other people who buy similar televisions.

Moreover, college education is a product most people consume only once. No matter how satisfied they are with their college education, the most people can do is recommend the school to family members or friends. Educational institutions are forced to spend considerable resources on consumers who have virtually no chance of being repeat customers. Although some of these expenditures create attributes that improve reputation and draw in future students and, for some, donations, others affect only current students.

Student Choice

Just as selective colleges choose among student applicants, many students have a choice of colleges and universities they might attend.

Students face a daunting set of decisions about whether, when, and where to continue their education after high school. The first question is whether to go to college at all. Many prospective students have no experience with higher education and may underestimate its value. The consumers are often young people whose desire for immediate gratification and undervaluing of future benefits may cause them to choose the job market over investing in themselves through education, even if this choice is less than optimal in the long run.

Then there are thousands of institutions to choose from. Most prospective students—or potential customers—are not able to make the kind of informed choices they make in other markets. Informed consumers are a necessary condition for the competitive economy that is supposed to create efficient outcomes. If consumer information is limited, markets will not operate efficiently because consumers may look for the cheapest supplier regardless of quality or conversely opt for the priciest and most prestigious supplier even if it is a poor fit for their needs. It is difficult for potential students (consumers) in this position to accurately weigh the costs and benefits of their purchases in advance of enrolling.

Students may also face different opportunities depending on their location. We noted in chapter 2 that states differ greatly in the number of higher education institutions within their borders. Many students commute, and even those who don't tend to prefer to go to a college near home. This geographic variation affects colleges' decision-making too. Universities in states with small populations of students may find it hard to maintain highly specialized programs or to impose very high admission standards because of limited numbers of potential applicants. To be sure, some top institutions have a strong national draw, but most places don't.

Familiar examples of market failure involving incomplete information include markets for medical care, where consumers must rely on suppliers for information about the need for services and the quality of those services. For a more mundane example, think about vacationers relying on brochures and testimonials to weigh the quality of a distant resort. But patients and tourists frequently have a choice about repeat visits—rarely a question for college students.

The federal government has put considerable effort into increasing the information available to students trying to choose a college. Each college is required to have a "net price calculator" on its website that provides a (very rough) estimate of how much students will have to pay if they enroll. The College Scorecard website provides information about the programs offered, share of applicants accepted, graduation rate, average annual cost, average earnings after graduation, typical student loan debt, and demographics of the student body. But even if they access this website, many students will have trouble knowing what to make of the information and figuring out how it should influence their decisions.

Consumers of education are unlikely to know exactly what outcomes they want, and they are not able to entirely appreciate the offerings until after they have already benefited from them. Even after students have completed their schooling, it is not a simple task to compare the value of one institution to another, or even the value of a college education to years spent in the labor force. The nonmonetary benefits are almost impossible to define fully, much less measure. But even the value of the short-term financial benefit of a specific educational experience for a particular individual is elusive, given the impossibility of controlled experiments and of sampling alternative choices. A full understanding of what education can do for one's life (beyond landing a first job) will develop over the lifetime of the student. It is not likely to be common among 18-year-old high school graduates.

These realities have significant implications for how educational institutions respond to consumer demand. For profit-maximizing firms in most industries, monitoring consumer preferences is vital, and modifying their offerings in accordance with changing tastes is important for survival. While educational institutions clearly must be responsive to student preferences to survive, if colleges go too far along this path, they may be at risk of failing to deliver the service that defines their mission. The familiar questions of whether students should take required courses and whether colleges should continue to offer relatively unpopular programs with intellectual justification are related to this phenomenon.

There is some danger in the current market for higher education that more and more institutions will cater to the short-run vocational training demands of students. Although these demands must be met, and although some institutions may perceive changing in this direction as the only means of survival, in the end, people are not likely to pay the high price of education for simple training. And liberal education, with its significant social value, could be allowed to disappear because 18-year-olds don't understand its importance.

The job of colleges and universities is to educate students and expand knowledge. The fundamental contract between college and student is that faculty and administrators will use their judgment and knowledge to make demands of students that will help them to learn as much as possible. Students cede much of their autonomy and sovereignty to the institutions in which they enroll. They agree to take the courses and meet the academic requirements prescribed by the institution. Students rely on the institution to make many of the decisions about what is best for them. If colleges and universities attempt to cater to the whims of their customers the way car dealers do, they will be unable to deliver the service that is their reason for being. Indeed, one core reason for relying on public and private nonprofit suppliers in higher education is to bolster the institutions' capacity to provide for students' educational needs instead of just "selling them" whatever they want.

Costs and Revenues Should Not Necessarily Dictate Decisions

In competitive markets, the consumer is supposed to be in charge. If a clothing store doesn't change its fashions to keep up with changing tastes, customers will shop elsewhere. Perhaps a college that fails to offer trendy classes will lose students to competing campuses. But arguing that student preferences may be cyclical and faddish, and that college enrollments may be affected by this reality, is not the same as arguing that colleges should tailor their curriculum to meet the latest fad.

It may be entirely reasonable that a college maintain its archaeology department even if it has very few majors, depending on the college's circumstances and mission. But that doesn't mean we should fail to understand that the department is likely to cost money and require a transfer of resources from other endeavors. Finding out that the revenues of the college would increase if all required courses were eliminated does not by itself imply that there should be radical curriculum reform. But it does mean that the cost of the requirements should be acknowledged and the source of funds to cover those costs should be identified.

Colleges must attract students to be able to expose them to the educational opportunities they offer. (A challenge the Archaeology Department needs to answer is just whom that department is serving if it has very few students. It could be the larger scholarly community if the department includes one or more strong scholars.) Ignoring student preferences and willingness to pay is not a viable option. Liberal arts educators may be deeply committed to the idea that this is the form of education that can best prepare people for a changing society and economy. But students must be open to this idea before they come to college to be convinced to enroll in these programs instead of more vocationally oriented training programs. In other words, consumer preferences—and the shaping of consumer preferences—must play a role in the planning process for educational institutions.

The reality is that a college cannot operate successfully if it does not attract an adequate student population. Elaborate athletic facilities and well-appointed dorm rooms are part of this effort at many residential colleges. Balancing the marketing of the institution and the tailoring of its offerings to student demand with the commitment of the faculty and administration to quality education based on their greater knowledge and experience is a challenge.

Selective Colleges

The selectivity of the admission process at many colleges and universities is also an important distinguishing characteristic. The goal is not to maximize *sales*. The quality of the educational product would likely be diluted by larger classes and less qualified students, and the institution's goal is to provide strong educational services—not to maximize revenues.

Many colleges and universities are unwilling to sell their product to everyone who is willing to pay. There are few firms in other industries that turn away customers who are willing to pay because they don't meet the admission standards. Moreover, some colleges and universities choose to enroll students who pay lower prices because they receive institutional grant aid, while they turn away people willing to pay the full sticker price. It is hard to image businesses selling products such as sofas or clothing turning away customers willing to pay the full price in favor of those paying only a fraction of the asking price. There are examples of industries where this may occur but would be deemed unethical—such as housing markets that exclude some demographic groups regardless of their ability to pay or restaurants that limit access. But selective colleges (a small minority of all colleges[1]) turn away potential customers who are able and willing to pay because of their lack of academic preparation. These colleges must market themselves to desirable students not only to gain tuition revenues, but also to ensure that they maintain the ability to provide high-quality education.

Summary

Colleges and universities are different from business firms in a variety of ways. They operate for the sake of providing educational opportunities rather than primarily out of financial motivation. The people who buy their services—the students—are an important input into the production process. The quality of education that students receive depends not only on the institution, but also on their own effort and abilities. It also depends on the characteristics of the other students. Colleges could not provide a reasonable quality of education if they judged each aspect of their operation on its ability to bring in revenues.

Despite their profound differences in mission and operation, colleges and universities operate within a market economy. The fact that most colleges are nonprofit doesn't mean they are not motivated to operate efficiently. Using more resources than necessary to, for example, run the registrar's office, will mean that there will be less money available to pay faculty. If faculty spend a lot of money going to conferences of questionable value, there will be less money to put into their pension funds. Maximizing the quality of education produced requires efficiency, just as maximizing profits does. Refusing to talk about efficiency is counterproductive.

To continue to be viable, institutions must operate efficiently and limit expenditures to the level of available resources. In the long run, ignoring the bottom line may be as harmful to the educational mission as focusing too narrowly on the bottom line. The unique characteristics of higher education do not mean that general economic principles do not apply. It may sometimes be useful to think of educational institutions as firms providing a product, of faculty and staff as inputs into a production process, and of students as utility-maximizing consumers. But there is considerable danger in this approach. The issue is not that it demeans the quality or importance of education to think of it as a commodity. Rather, the conditions of production and consumption of higher education are, in some ways, unique. Ignoring this uniqueness can lead to some shortsighted decisions in the supposed interest of efficiency.

CHAPTER FIVE

How Should We Think about the Compensation Budget?

SALARIES, COMPENSATION, AND FACULTY STATUS

Diane, a long-time English Department chair who recently became Dean of the Faculty, is grappling with complaints about faculty salaries. She and her English Department colleagues have long resented the fact that their pay is so much lower than that of faculty in most of the other departments. Now, for the first time, she is about to hire a newly minted PhD in computer science at a salary that exceeds that of some full professors in the English Department.

The Computer Science Department has been searching for this position for three years, and they are very excited about the young woman they have found. But she has competing offers, and they are quite sure they will lose her if their offer is not high enough. The College will be a better place with this new faculty member—and with a satisfied and dedicated English Department. Everyone understands that salary differentials by field are inevitable. But when are they just too much?

A WIDE RANGE of debates on campus relate to compensation. Sometimes the focus is on salaries, sometimes on benefits. Advocates for faculty may or may not include non-instructional staff in their efforts. Concerns about faculty status, such as reliance on part-time and non-tenure-track faculty are also about a form of compensation—more broadly defined and unique to faculty.

Salaries versus Compensation

Annual debates on campus about salary increases could be improved by a clearer distinction between salaries and total compensation. Compensation includes both salary—current cash income—and benefits such as health care, retirement contributions, and life insurance. For full-time faculty members, salary makes up about 75 to 80 percent of compensation on average, and benefits account for 20 to 25 percent.[1]

Some of the non-salary benefits received by faculty and staff are in the form of cash, and others are in-kind benefits. Contributions to retirement funds are cash paid out by the institution and credited to employees now that become income in the future. Health insurance is an in-kind benefit that will be used to different extents by different employees. The institution has discretion over some benefits. It can alter the amount it contributes to pension funds, the percentage of health care premiums covered, or the amount of life insurance it provides. But it has no choice about the contributions it makes to the Social Security and unemployment compensation funds in the names of employees.

It is easy for employees to think only in terms of salary, since it is the size of their paychecks that has the most immediate effect on their daily lives. On the other hand, financial officers tend to focus primarily on total compensation, since salary and benefits affect the budget similarly. Increases in the cost of health coverage for employees must be offset either by decreases in other expenditures or by increases in revenue. If insurance companies raise their prices, employers will view this as an increase in compensation costs and may want to cut salaries (or slow salary increases) to compensate for it. But employees aren't better off because rates went up, and they are likely to resist seeing higher insurance costs as a solid reason to cut their salaries.

Keeping Up with the Cost of Living

It is common for college and university employees—like other workers—to seek salary increases at least commensurate with the rate of growth in consumer prices. This is reasonable since no one wants to lose purchasing power and experience a decline in their standard of living. But while most people realize that the cost of living differs quite a bit in different locations—a given salary will support a higher standard of living in rural Kansas than in San Francisco—it is also true that the CPI *rises* at different rates in different places. For example, between 2015 and 2020, when the CPI rose by 9 percent, prices rose by 6 percent in the Philadelphia area and by 16 percent in the San Francisco area.

If average salaries on campus rise with the CPI, the real standard of living will remain constant. Average incomes don't always rise faster than prices. Real median earnings for faculty in the United States fell from 2007 to 2011 and did not reach their previous peak again until 2016. Nonetheless, in 2019, median earnings were 16 percent higher after adjusting for inflation than in 2009, and 13 percent higher than in 1999.[2] While earnings levels in the economy fluctuate with the business cycle, the normal expectation is that wages will rise above inflation over time, reflecting growth in productivity. Faculty and university staff would be quite distressed if their purchasing power did not increase, and they were able to buy only the same goods and services that were within the reach of their grandparents. As we noted earlier, academic workers, like barbers, do not generally benefit from the growing productivity technology provides in other fields like manufacturing. To enable faculty and staff incomes to grow in line with other professions, the real cost of providing education must rise. The goal for faculty on campus is for salaries to rise more rapidly than the CPI. But trustees, administrators, and (for public institutions) legislators may worry more about salary increases putting upward pressure on tuition.

Average Salaries and Individual Salaries

The math of tracking individual salaries and average salary by rank is not simple. In a typical year a college will experience the retirement of some long-time faculty with relatively high salaries at the same time new assistant professors arrive with low starting salaries. It's mathematically possible for every faculty member at a college to get a raise while the average faculty salary (or the total salary bill) remains constant.

More generally, as older workers retire and new workers are hired, continuing employees can see their wages rise more rapidly than the average salary. Individuals also see their earnings rise more rapidly than the average salary as they move up the ladder of seniority.

Confusion may also arise over the difference between changes in the compensation budget and in the typical salary. An increase in the compensation pool could be driven either by more dollars being directed toward continuing employees or by an increase in the total number of employees.

Personnel costs constitute more than half of campus operating expenses at both public and private institutions (on average, 61 percent at public and 55 percent at private nonprofit institutions in 2018–19). A large fraction of personnel costs, often more than half, are for non-faculty personnel. Non-cash benefits make up an average of 28 percent of total compensation at public and 18 percent at private nonprofit institutions. At for-profit institutions, just under half (49 percent) of spending goes to compensation, and only 6 percent of that compensation goes to benefits.[3] If other expenditures—on technology, energy, or financial aid, for example—rise more rapidly than the CPI, salaries can be maintained in real terms only if revenues rise more rapidly than the CPI.

These subtle distinctions aren't just "academic"—they are eminently practical. When staff and faculty are working to achieve agreement with administrators on compensation policy, it's vital to be sure they are speaking the same language and aiming at the same targets.

Variation in Faculty Salaries

Faculty salaries vary dramatically both from campus to campus and within institutions. In 2020–21, the average salary for full professors at private nonprofit doctoral universities was $202,199. At private master's universities, it was $116,426. At public universities, these figures were $164,020 and $102,450, respectively. At one fifth of all doctoral universities, the average salary for assistant professors was more than $103,070. In the lowest fifth it was less than $75,944.[4]

In salary discussions on campus, the focus is frequently on how faculty on one campus compare to faculty on another campus. A few words of caution are in order about these comparisons. The question of whether to compare average salaries across campuses or average salaries within ranks across campuses provides a simple example. Suppose College A and College B have identical salary structures. Average salaries at all ranks are the same. Now College A promotes 10 associate professors to the rank of full professor. College B makes no promotions. Average salaries will go up at College A because of the premium attached to rank. Faculty at College B may complain that they have fallen behind. However, because College A has many new full professors, their average salary for full professors falls, as does the average salary for associate professors, since the most senior members of this group have moved on. So, when comparing by ranks, College A finds it has fallen behind College B, and the faculty may complain. A development that really has nothing to do with the generosity of salaries has now created dissatisfaction on both campuses.

Variation in salaries within a faculty can also cause tensions.

Average salaries for male faculty members are higher than those for female faculty members. Average salaries for women at the instructor rank at public master's universities are 98 percent of male salaries. Average salaries for female full professors at independent private doctoral universities are 89 percent of those for men. Overall gender gaps in average salaries are larger than those within ranks, because men are more likely to be at higher ranks. For example, at public doctoral universities, the average salary for female faculty is 81 percent of the average for men. But at every rank, women earn at least 90 percent as much as men.[5]

Within institutions, faculty in different fields may have very different salary levels. In 2019–20, the average salaries for full professors in English Language and Literature ranged from $71,452 at two-year institutions and $79,584 at baccalaureate colleges to $102,814 at research doctoral universities. For assistant professors the range was from $57,037 to $67,466. The average salaries for full professors in Engineering ranged from $76,360 at two-year institutions and $91,405 at baccalaureate colleges to $142,933 at research doctoral universities. For assistant professors the range was from $60,670 to $93,284. Faculty in the legal professions earned even more.[6]

These disciplinary differences are largely explained by the realities of supply and demand. Increased demand for certain types of labor puts upward pressure on wages in those occupations. The decision to pay economists more than philosophers does not imply a judgment that the contribution of one group is any more or less important than the contribution of the other group. But economists have more employment opportunities outside the academy than philosophers do. In other words, the demand for their services is higher. This means that if the college offers them a low wage, they are likely to choose to work elsewhere. Philosophers with comparable qualifications for teaching and research are not in great demand outside the academy, so more of them will be willing to accept the relatively low salaries offered.

This explanation for salary differentials has nothing to do with differential merit or effort. The economists are not working harder. They are not necessarily teaching more students or adding more in any way to the output of the institution. This is a situation in which those who focus on what seems fair and those who focus on the dictates of the market are likely to reach different conclusions.

The salary differentials between assistant professors and associate and full professors are another area in which dissatisfaction is likely to arise. Again, supply and demand may collide with common notions of equity. In this case it is the supply side where the differences are clearest. Tenured faculty sometimes receive competing offers from other institutions, but the average senior faculty member at most institutions has few options but to stay put. The institution does not need to increase full professor wages rapidly to prevent the ranks from being depleted.

There is an active market for faculty at the entry level that puts competitive pressure on the salaries of assistant professors. This is not the case for senior faculty (except at top research universities). Institutions are more likely to lose young people by offering noncompetitive salaries than to lose those valued members of the community who have been around for years and are central to the functioning of the institution.

Again, the dictates of the market work in a direction that is potentially inconsistent with common notions of equity—and with paying people in accordance with their value to the institution. This efficiency argument for a narrowing range of salaries for faculty by age and rank—paying entering faculty relatively well to attract them to campus—does, however, have limits. If insufficient salary differentials—or insufficient rates of salary growth—damage faculty morale, or even push those senior faculty with some mobility to leave—they could seriously affect the quality of the education the institution provides.

Both equity and efficiency considerations should motivate the compensation structure. It may be most efficient to pay generous starting salaries but to hold down salaries for senior faculty who have limited opportunities outside the institution. However, equity considerations may well dictate more generous policies toward senior faculty who provide high levels of campus service and who constitute the core of the academic community. Moreover, administrators who are too quick to respond to those individuals or departments who are the "squeakiest wheels" may wind up souring the atmosphere of the place.

Faculty—at least at institutions requiring PhDs—are frequently hired in a national market. After graduate school, many are willing to relocate to find a good job. Noninstructional staff are more likely to be in local labor markets. Colleges hiring support staff and maintenance workers are competing with nearby industries, not with colleges around the country. This difficulty compounds the distinctions in campus roles and required training in creating challenges for the development of equitable compensation structures within college communities.

Nonsalary Compensation

There is no objective answer to the question of what a fair level of compensation is. In addressing the issue, however, it is important to consider some factors in addition to salary levels. First, compensation includes not only salary but also benefits. Health care, pensions, life insurance, and other benefits do not appear in salary figures, but they constitute about a quarter of employee compensation on college campuses and significantly affect standards of living. There is a wide range in the benefits received by college employees, but they are likely to receive benefit packages more generous than those offered in the for-profit sector. In 2020, 71 percent of employees in private industry and state and local governments had access to any employer-sponsored retirement benefits. This included 86 percent of those in management, professional, and related occupations. Only a portion of these workers receive contributions from their employers. Some of these contributions require a match from employees. Similar shares of employees have access to medical care benefits. On average, employees pay 20 percent of the premiums for single-person coverage and 33 percent for family coverage. Sixty percent of employees have access to life insurance benefits.[7] In contrast, 94 percent of full-time faculty members have access to institutional health insurance, and a similar share have retirement benefits.[8] In other words, benefits make up a larger share of the compensation of faculty members than of employees in other industries.

The job definitions of faculty members also vary widely across institutions and departments. Few faculty members would view a job requiring them to teach six courses each year as equivalent to a job requiring four courses each year for the same salary and benefits. Administrators often use teaching "load" as a sort of currency that can convince a professor to take on a necessary assignment. For example, the faculty member chosen to chair a department might be offered a course "off" in exchange for the added administrative work. Research expectations also create very different job characteristics.

Another aspect of compensation that is too easily ignored is what economists call **nonpecuniary benefits**. Some jobs pay higher salaries because they require unpleasant or dangerous activities. Most people would have to be paid more to be sanitation workers than to work in a clean and pleasant environment. College campuses frequently have high-quality fitness centers and other types of facilities available to employees. Faculty members in particular are likely to be on nine- or ten-month contracts. Although many faculty members may be unable to easily supplement their earnings over the summer, they benefit from the flexible academic schedule. At many institutions they also enjoy regular paid sabbatical leaves, a phenomenon virtually unknown outside the academy. Full-time faculty have an unusual amount of autonomy both in designing their work agendas and in allocating their time. The nature of the academic enterprise would be dramatically transformed if faculty members were required to track their time the way lawyers must when billing clients. Probably most notable is that the tenure system provides some college faculty with a highly unusual level of job security. In other words, just comparing dollars and cents may give an inaccurate picture of comparative compensation levels.

Staffing Structure

Compensation levels for tenured and tenure-track faculty tell only part of the story. About half of the instructional staff at public and private nonprofit colleges and universities (and more than 80 percent at for-profit institutions) are employed part time. Two-thirds of instructional staff at public two-year colleges are part time, compared with 36 percent of those at public four-year and 48 percent at private nonprofit four-year institutions.[9] Although there are exceptions, most part-time faculty are not considered for tenurable appointments, implying that they experience more job insecurity as well as generally lower pay than full-timers,

The share of faculty employed full time declined steadily from 78 percent in 1970 to 64 percent in 1990 and 50 percent in 2011. Since then, the trend has reversed, and 54 percent of faculty were full time in 2018 (see figure 5.1).

Despite the concerns about administrative bloat reducing the resources available for faculty appointments, faculty are not a declining portion of college and university staff. The share of employees who are instructional staff (excluding graduate assistants) has risen over time in both public and private nonprofit institutions. (See box on administrative bloat in chapter 6). But while the number of instructional staff has grown faster than the number of administrative staff, that is not true of budgets, where

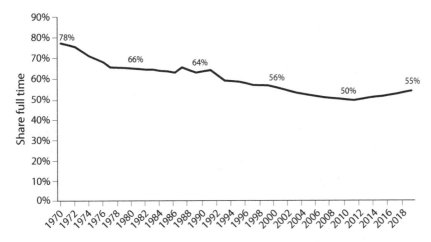

FIGURE 5.1. Share of Faculty in Degree-Granting Postsecondary Institutions
Employed Full Time, Fall 1970 to Fall 2019
Source: US Department of Education, *Digest of Education Statistics 2020*, Table 315.10

instructional staff spending has grown more slowly than spending on other staff. This has come about in part because more skilled and expensive professional staff have replaced lower paid typists and clerks. This development inevitably increases the compensation going to noninstructional staff.

Tenure

Tenure is not generally thought of as a part of compensation, but long-term job security is a form of compensation. Skepticism about tenure is longstanding. In 1999, James Carlin, a past chair of the Massachusetts Board of Education, wrote: "Tenure rewards the lazy and incompetent. Its costs are enormous."[10]

Questions from the public, from state legislatures, and from boards of trustees about the practice of faculty tenure are increasingly common and increasingly critical. Proposals have been made in several states to eliminate tenure at public colleges. Because it is difficult to find other industries in which employees have the level of job security granted to tenured faculty, it is not surprising that the wisdom of the system appears dubious to many observers. Yet there is probably no other subject that angers faculty more than the allegation that tenure results in a large fraction of faculty "retiring on the job," "going through the motions," and so on.

Historically, the case for tenure has been deeply entwined with the argument for academic freedom, about which economists have no special claim to expertise. Nonetheless, an understanding of the academic labor market and how it is affected by the tenure system is a critical underpinning for any discussion of tenure. Given the weight of compensation in college and university budgets, it is impossible to expect that those responsible for the bottom line will not insist that the financial implications of the system be considered.

Colleges and universities that rely on the institution of tenure as a major component of their personnel system must make unusually long term, and therefore risky, commitments. For individual tenure candidates, the institution must make a prediction about how well someone's career will develop. (These risks have become greater since higher education's exemption from the prohibition on mandatory retirement age ended in 1994.[11]) But beyond the risks of individual appointments going awry, universities must weigh the risk that the structure of higher education will change in ways that make long-term employment in its current form obsolete. From an economic point of view, colleges that operate a tenure system are "tying their own hands" by giving up personnel tools that other employers use.

There are a variety of realities not related to academic freedom or ideology that might cause colleges and universities to lay off some number of senior-level faculty members in the absence of a tenure system. Like any enterprise, colleges and universities face fluctuations in the demand for their services. Changing demographics and economic conditions can have a dramatic effect on the number of applications a college receives. It is possible that in the absence of tenure, a significant number of faculty would lose their jobs during periods of low enrollment. On most college campuses, this is a startling idea.

Of course, in other industries, layoffs are an accepted reality. Profit-making companies have considerable discretion to replace workers who do not carry their weight. This makes it difficult for outsiders to understand why academics should be so protected from market forces. However, theoretical models of labor markets that describe the demanders of labor as constantly finding the most productive workers at the lowest possible cost are unrealistic.

While the formal protections of job security are higher in academia than elsewhere, in practice most Americans have relatively stable employment. The costs of turnover, which include search and training processes, are high. On average, workers have been with their current employers for about five years. For workers ages 55 to 64, the median is about 10 years.[12] More than half of the 3 percent of workers who leave their jobs each month do so voluntarily.[13] In other words, while tenure provides unique protection, and there is likely less turnover among faculty than there would be in the absence of tenure, workers elsewhere are not let go as often as the justifiable focus on the hardship this process can cause might suggest.

Still, the security of tenure is unique, and it is not surprising that it is valuable to academics, even beyond issues of academic freedom. The particularly specialized training of college and university faculty creates special circumstances in their labor market. The difficulty of applying the skill set of an art history professor to any other type of job makes it quite reasonable that faculty are willing to sacrifice some current earnings in exchange for job security.

A distinctive feature of universities and colleges that contributes to the value of tenure is that faculty, and especially tenured faculty, generally play a significant managerial role in academic personnel decisions. Disciplinary specialization can make it hard for those in other fields to judge the quality of a faculty member's research or teaching. Faculty whose jobs are in continuing jeopardy might be reluctant to encourage the hiring or retention of higher quality faculty who might threaten their own future. It's also to the long-run benefit of the university to have faculty who can plan on a lasting future at the institution.[14]

There are some strong efficiency arguments for continuous employment from the perspective of the institution. This is no doubt true in other industries as well, but perhaps not to the same extent because of the centrality of personal interaction in the role of faculty. Experience and attachment to the institution have a significant impact on an individual's contribution. Faculty members do not just teach courses. They know the particular students at their schools, and they work closely with their colleagues in a variety of ways. There is relatively little turnover in most college faculties. A dramatic change in employment relationships could change that pattern, diminishing the collaborative nature of the educational environment.

In other industries, where there is usually more of a hierarchy and more variety in the jobs available to individual employees, the most competent employees are likely to be promoted frequently. Those whose performance is more mediocre may stay put or be moved to jobs with less responsibility. About 9 percent of employees are promoted each year, with an average accompanying wage increase of 17 percent.[15] This sort of job change is rarely available to academics once they reach the full professor rank. Tenure, with its stringent one-time evaluation process, is a system much more suited to academia than to other industries.

Many of the arguments against tenure are based on the difficulty of enforcing continuing productivity among tenured faculty. Economic theories of the labor market are often based on the idea that employers are unwilling to pay workers more than the amount their productivity contributes to the enterprise. A profit-making organization cannot survive if it is losing money because of unproductive employees. But most colleges are not profit-making organizations. And on many campuses, it is possible to find some number of tenured faculty who do not pull their weight. This inefficiency is seen by some as an argument for abandoning the tenure system.

As discussed in chapter 3, measuring productivity in higher education is not clear-cut. If a professor teaches poorly but students continue to register for her classes out of necessity, how is the decline in productivity observed? If too many faculty members are in this category, enrollments will surely decline. But students who take these courses still get their credits and graduate, so a few burned-out instructors may not, in fact, have a measurable economic effect on the institution.

Moreover, it is not at all clear that tenure has a negative impact on faculty productivity. By allowing them the luxury of focusing on their role in a particular institution, rather than on more widely marketable, less institution-specific activities, tenure tends to foster an unusually engaged and dedicated employee community. While tenured faculty tend to teach less, they often spend more time on administrative tasks.[16]

Another interesting perspective on the productivity impact of tenure comes from the theory of *x-efficiency* in labor markets. Theorists have long recognized that maximum productivity may not result from maximum exposure to market forces. Workers who are satisfied, who feel appreciated, and who enjoy a comfortable, rewarding work environment are likely to be more productive than those who are treated poorly and are frustrated with their circumstances. Higher wages and better working conditions may directly increase worker productivity.

Tenure and the accompanying sense of belonging in an institution are likely to have a strong positive effect on faculty commitment to their teaching, their professional work, and their service to the college or university community. In the absence of tenure, faculty focus would be much more on professional accomplishments in the interest of mobility than on activities that directly affect students and the rest of the college community.

Despite the difficulty of defining and measuring productivity for faculty, the academy has developed an elaborate and thorough evaluation process for tenure. Most institutions put considerable resources into evaluating individual faculty members in their sixth year of employment. The probability that a faculty member whose performance is adequate but not spectacular will lose his or her job after the probationary period is significantly greater than the probability that an employee with a similar level of performance in another industry would be fired. It may well also be significantly higher than it would be under any sort of contract system that might replace tenure. Studies have found that institutions without tenure have no more turnover than those with tenure.[17] The lifetime character of the tenure contract makes the scrutiny applied much more intense.

The tenure system does appear to decrease mobility at higher levels in the academic labor market. In the corporate world, it is not uncommon for management level personnel to move from one company to another. A typical pattern of career success for executive and managerial personnel is "moving through the ranks" at a number of firms. A somewhat similar pattern holds for some executives in higher education, as a professor may move from being a divisional dean at one university to a become a provost at another and might even be appointed president at a third institution. This is a much less common pattern of advancement for faculty outside the administrative ranks except at the top research universities.

Under the tenure system, we wait for unproductive workers to retire. This means that there are fewer openings for senior-level faculty. At the same time, the fact that most senior faculty expect to be there "for the duration" means that their personal success is deeply connected to the success of the institution where they are employed, reenforcing their loyalty and commitment.

A reform that some have advocated is to add college and university faculty to the short list of professions that continue to have mandatory retirement (airline pilots being the most prominent example.) Combining academic tenure with open-ended employment adds considerably to the burdens of tenure. Achieving such a change would require an act of Congress, and of course could only apply to future hires.

Avoiding the debate about tenure could have serious negative results. Failure to face the labor market implications of tenure head on may cause the system to wither without any conscious decisions to repeal it. An open dialogue on the subject with the possibility of some modifications carefully designed with the interests of academic freedom and faculty autonomy at the core may be preferable to the gradual undermining of the system most faculty view as fundamental to their professional work.

Alternative Arrangements

The discussion above has not mentioned unions, which have been a growing force in US higher education. Long prevalent among noninstructional staff, collective bargaining has become more widespread among graduate students who serve as instructors and teaching assistants, and in the swelling ranks of adjunct and non-tenure-track faculty. Tenured and tenure-track faculty often play roles in hiring, promotion, and other governance policies that may be seen as making them "managerial" employees who are not eligible for unionization. Where they exist (more often in public than in private institutions), faculty unions may restrict the channels through which faculty participate in governance. They also bring more formal structure to bargaining and clearer grievance procedures, making salary and compensation structures and processes quite different from those at other colleges and universities.

As discussed above, in recent years an increasing number of faculty are part-time or full-time without job security. They are not eligible for consideration for tenure. This development is of considerable concern to faculty interested in preserving tenure. It is a natural market response to the institution of tenure, however. In the interest of keeping compensation costs down and of avoiding long-term commitments in an uncertain, competitive environment, institutions are finding ways to hire people to whom they are not required to make a lifetime commitment. It is possible to argue that the inflexibility of the tenure system makes it very attractive for the administration to find alternative employment arrangements. That said, there is no doubt that these arrangements pose a threat both to the practice of tenure and the quality of the educational environment as traditionally defined.

The share of full-time faculty with tenure ranges from 37 percent at private nonprofit master's universities and 38 percent at private doctoral universities to 48 percent at private baccalaureate colleges and 52 percent at public master's universities, as figure 5.2 shows. Tenure-track faculty account for another 16 to 24 percent of full-time faculty in each sector. The rest are not on the tenure track, either because their institution does not have a tenure system or because they were hired into a position outside the tenure system in place. The share in this situation ranges from 25 percent at public master's universities and 31 percent at private baccalaureate colleges to 46 percent at public associate colleges and private doctoral universities.

In addition to the increasing reliance on part-time and adjunct faculty, a variety of modifications to traditional faculty employment patterns are developing. Alternatives include term-limited contracts, and robust post-tenure review with consequences for weak performance. These changes are rooted in concern over the cost and inflexibility of tenure. But the question of whether the tenure system increases the cost of compensation for institutions is not

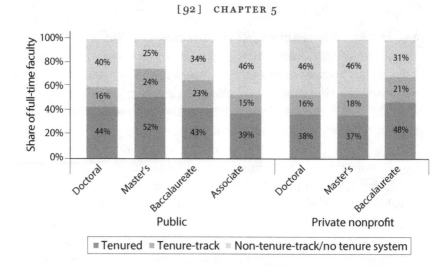

FIGURE 5.2. Share of Full-Time Faculty Who Are Tenured, on the Tenure Track, or Not Eligible for Tenure, 2018–19

Note: Faculty may be not eligible for tenure either because their institutions do not have a tenure system or because they were not hired within the tenure system.

Source: *Chronicle of Higher Education*, "Percentages of Full-Time Faculty Members Who Were Non-Tenure Track."

straightforward. On one hand, colleges and universities are not free to replace higher-paid senior faculty with lower-paid junior faculty at will or even in order to increase the quality of education offered. On the other hand, faculty salaries are surely lower than they would be in a labor market characterized by more competition among institutions for faculty. The relatively high salaries of the small number of "stars" in academia, who do in fact experience competitive bidding for their services, provide some clues about the direction in which a free market might lead. Simple statements about how we can't afford the tenure system may not be well informed. And a failure to understand the very significant role tenure plays in the compensation of faculty can make faculty feel under-rewarded.

Summary

Faculty and staff salaries are a frequent point of tension on college campuses. Comparisons with others on campus and with people in similar positions at other institutions can be meaningful but are fraught with measurement difficulties. The most obvious problem is that similar salaries can correspond to quite different levels of compensation, depending on benefit packages, as well as to very different job descriptions. Anyone involved in campus discussions about compensation increases over time or relative salary structures should be sure to carefully consider all the factors in play, including the range of labor markets in which the institution operates.

Questions about tenure—about the wisdom of the system and about threats to its preservation—are central to discussions about the nature of the academic enterprise, but also to discussions about compensation. An increasing share of faculty appointments are outside the tenure system. The pros and cons of this trend deserve attention as part of deliberations about compensation.

What about Adjuncts?

The legislation Bernie Sanders introduced in the Senate in an effort to make public colleges tuition free for all students included a provision requiring that 75 percent of classes at participating institutions be taught by full-time tenured or tenure-track faculty.[18] Aside from raising significant questions about the role of the federal government in regulating colleges and universities, this standard would have required dramatic changes in staffing.

According to the American Association of University Professors, in 2016, 73 percent of instructional positions (including about 20 percent filled by graduate students) across postsecondary institutions were nontenure track.[19] Faculty members hired off the tenure track may be full time or part time, and their contracts may be for one semester, one academic year, or longer. Most part-time faculty members are hired off the tenure track and are called "adjunct" or "contingent" faculty. But many non-tenure-track faculty teach full time, usually on contracts of one academic year or longer.

Aside from questions about academic freedom and the fundamental arguments for faculty tenure, objections to the growing reliance on adjuncts are rooted in concerns over their compensation and working conditions, as well as in questions about the impact on students.

Arguments for hiring part-time and short-term faculty include the flexibility they provide for changes in curriculum and in the demand for particular courses and fields, as well as the cost savings involved in their lower salaries and, frequently, reduced benefits. From an administrator's perspective, lower costs per unit mean lower tuition and/or more resources for other expenses. Hiring more tenure-track faculty and/or raising the compensation levels of contingent faculty would require finding more money somewhere.

On the other hand, the low pay, logistical difficulties, and lack of status and voice within the institution experienced by most contingent faculty surely limit their ability to fully contribute to their institutions and may provoke questions about the university's values.

The evidence about the implications of relying on nontenure-track faculty is mixed. Some research finds that hiring a larger share of contingent non-tenure-track faculty does not, in fact, strengthen the financial health of vulnerable public universities. It is possible that the lower costs are offset by higher spending in other areas such as administrative costs, student support, higher salaries, or research support for the smaller share of tenured faculty who are central to the institutional mission. Too much erosion of the tenured faculty could reduce the institution's ability to bring in research funding or even affect applications for admissions. Hearn and Burns (2021), focusing on public master's and doctoral universities, find no measurable relationship between the extent to which financially weak institutions shift to part-time and non-tenure-track faculty and changes in their financial health.[20]

There is also conflicting evidence about the impact of reliance on contingent faculty on student outcomes. A lack of supportive policies, practices, and resources may hamper their ability to utilize effective educational practices. There is some evidence of lower student learning and persistence.[21] But others find that because of the poor classroom performance of some tenured faculty, contingent faculty are, on average, more effective teachers than tenured and tenure-track faculty, at least in introductory courses.[22] Practices concerning the treatment of adjuncts, notably their job security and institutional status, vary enormously, so generalizations are hazardous.

People seek out, or sometimes grudgingly accept, positions as adjuncts for a variety of reasons. Professional artists, designers, writers, accountants, and others in similar professions may find teaching part time a valuable way to supplement their incomes, and they may also enjoy the opportunity to teach. Retired faculty may find part-time teaching a rewarding way to stay involved in work they value or may need to supplement retirement income. In some academic fields, students pursue PhD degrees because they love their subject and are passionate about teaching but are not interested in the research demands of a tenure-track position.

In contrast, there are a significant number of people who pursue the PhD with the aim of becoming tenured faculty who find they have to settle for adjunct positions because the supply of new PhDs greatly exceeds the number of tenure-track positions available. There is irony in the fact that some universities find themselves on both the supply and demand sides of the market for adjunct faculty.

Trade-offs in relying more on contingent faculty likely include the advantages of increasing flexibility and reduced costs, at least in the short run, versus morale and institutional commitment—and possibly educational quality. Improving the working conditions and status of non-tenure-track faculty is almost certain to have a positive impact both on educational quality and the sense of equity among the faculty. But higher salaries and benefits are in tension with one of the central motivations for hiring these instructors—lowering costs to facilitate some combination of higher compensation for tenured and tenure-track faculty and lower tuition and/or more generous financial aid for students.

CHAPTER SIX

Do We Really Have to Cut the Budget?

In 2020, when the coronavirus pandemic was hitting colleges and universities hardest, budget cuts were pervasive. Startling headlines became commonplace:

"Colleges Slash Budgets in the Pandemic, With 'Nothing Off-Limits'"[1]

"Colleges Lower the Boom on Retirement Plans"[2]

"Harvard to Impose a Salary and Hiring Freeze due to Fallout from Coronavirus Outbreak"[3]

According to the 2021 Faculty Compensation Survey from the American Association of University Professors:[4]

- *Nearly 60 percent of institutions surveyed implemented salary freezes or reductions.*
- *About 30 percent eliminated or reduced some form of fringe benefits.*
- *Over 5 percent did not reappoint or terminated contracts for at least some tenure-line faculty.*
- *Over 20 percent did not renew contracts or terminated contracts for at least some non-tenure-track faculty.*
- *Almost 10 percent implemented furloughs for at least some faculty.*
- *Over 50 percent took some other action for tenure-line faculty. The most common action described was some type of early retirement program.*

- *Almost 30 percent took some other action for non-tenure-line faculty.*

Not surprisingly, these moves caused tensions on many campuses.[5] Some of these cuts reflected long-developing problems. Colleges don't cut a large share of their programs and lay off significant numbers of tenured faculty to solve temporary problems.

NO AMOUNT OF informed discussion is likely to put everyone on the same page about the urgency of cuts or the priorities for preserving the status quo and/or funding innovations. But deeper understanding of how funds are spent, the limits on revenues, and what the trade-offs are can help. And better communication and more inclusive decision-making processes can lead to better grounded conclusions, in addition to mitigating anger and resentment.

Addressing skepticism about the need for budget cuts and grappling with where the sacrifices should be if they are in fact necessary will always be challenging. But a thorough and transparent examination of the relevant aspects of the institution's circumstances will help. A few examples follow. These questions can shed light on whether cuts are warranted on your campus, and why.

When Does a Hiring Freeze Make Sense?

If the trustees and administrators see a need to restrain spending in the short run, they may be seeking ways to limit the impact on current employees. A hiring freeze will reduce the total number of faculty and staff at the college (or at least prevent it from growing). That can make it less likely that individual compensation levels will have to decline.

But a hiring freeze is temporary. It is impossible to refrain permanently from replacing departing faculty and staff or even to avoid creating any new positions. It is possible that hiring new faculty in the midst of the pandemic, when other institutions are postponing their hiring, would allow the college to attract better faculty with less salary competition than if they waited a year or two. Paying the salary for a new hire for a little longer might be well worth the long-term benefits.

Questions to ask:

- Is the goal of the freeze just to postpone hiring or to rethink the need for all the positions in question?
- What are the costs of leaving a position vacant? Will class sizes rise? Will current workers end up putting in a lot of overtime? Or might some restructuring lead to longer-term doubts about whether the position is actually necessary?
- Is the institution giving up a valuable hiring opportunity in the interest of a relatively small saving?

Why Are Retirement Benefits an Easy Target for Cuts?

During the coronavirus pandemic, many institutions reduced or eliminated their contributions to employee retirement funds. These cuts reduce compensation just as a salary cut would. Although salaries are frequently frozen, colleges and universities rarely cut them. (However, in 2020, top administrators at some institutions made prominent announcements about cutting their own salaries.) One explanation for the difference is that salary cuts are more painful in the moment. A cut in take-home pay will hit the household budget immediately. For most people, smaller retirement assets won't be felt for years to come.

A compelling argument for this choice—if indeed cuts to compensation are inevitable—is that employees could choose to add to their own retirement accounts to replace lost employer contributions. They can choose to bear the pain today instead of tomorrow.

But an understanding of compound interest should be part of the calculation. An $80,000-a-year employee whose employer contribution to retirement falls by 3 percentage points for just one year will lose $2,400. If that $2,400 earned a return of 5 percent per year for 30 years, it would become almost $10,000. So, the loss is not trivial.

Questions to ask:

- What share of the institution's operating budget is employee compensation?
- Why does employee compensation have to be cut? Could revenues from the endowment or from tuition be increased instead? Could cuts come from other parts of the budget?

- If the institution must spend less on compensation, should it decrease compensation for individual employees and/or reduce the number of employees, through layoffs, voluntary responses to new retirement incentives, or leaving positions open?
- If individual compensation is going to take a hit, should it be through salaries, retirement benefits, reduced contributions to health coverage, or other benefits?
- Which cuts will be easiest to restore when the financial situation looks up? Which are likely to be permanent?

Cuts to Graduate Programs

During the pandemic, some universities paused admissions to some of their graduate programs. Master's programs frequently make money for the institution because of the tuition revenues they bring in. Doctoral students are more likely to receive fellowships. Some may be funded by outside sources, but many, particularly in the humanities and social sciences, are essentially awarded tuition waivers from the university, sometimes accompanied by stipends to cover nontuition expenses. But many graduate students teach undergraduates, relieving instructional budget pressures. Those programs that are costly to operate but bring in little to no revenue are most vulnerable.

It is also worth noting that many observers argue that the United States produces too many PhDs.[6] If they are right, perhaps these pauses would be advisable even absent a budget crisis.

Question to ask:

- How were the departments whose graduate admissions were cut chosen?
- Is the plan to pause admissions for a year and then to go back to the previous class size?
- Which graduate programs bring in net revenues and which are subsidized by the university?
- What is the employment history of recent graduates of the programs being cut?
- What are the implications of the proposed cuts for the racial/ethnic breakdown of the graduate student body?

- How well do the programs under scrutiny fit the mission of the university, as understood by the campus community and by the trustees?
- Why are graduate students so important to the faculty who teach them?
- How will a shrinking pool of graduate students affect the cost and quality of undergraduate teaching?

Deferred Maintenance

Some cuts, such as those to employee compensation, bring immediate pain. Others may seem painless at the moment but create longer-term problems. Just as families can wait another year or two to buy a new car when their budgets are tight, colleges and universities can wait another year or two to replace vehicles, computers, or lab equipment. But if problems such as the deterioration of buildings are allowed to accumulate, they can become more serious and lead to expensive crises down the road.

It is worth noting that deferring maintenance is in a sense like drawing extra money from the endowment. In either case, near-term pain is eased by reducing the value of the college's assets. The decline in financial wealth in the case of an endowment draw may be more immediately visible, but the decline in physical wealth associated with deferred maintenance may end up being more costly.

If these expenses always go to the bottom of the list because they don't seem like emergencies—and they don't hit personal pocketbooks the way cuts to compensation do—the list of deferred items will grow unmanageably long. And some of them will turn into emergencies.

As in most other areas, priorities are likely to differ among people with different responsibilities. Admissions staff are intensely aware of the campus' aesthetic appeal to visitors. Science faculty need up-to-date equipment not only for their own work, but to attract new faculty. Facilities staff will be aware of the wiring and plumbing at risk of giving out at any time.

Questions to ask:

- How do the low interest rates that may be available during an economic downturn balance immediate financial pressures combined with uncertainty about future enrollments and tuition revenues in decisions about postponing building plans?

- Are the modernization projects on the agenda necessary to maintain the safety and functionality of campus buildings? How will postponing them affect the educational experience? The institution's ability to attract students?
- Has the institution developed a sound approach to balancing immediate and targeted benefits (salary increases, new computers for faculty and staff) with longer-term benefits to the community as a whole (new roofs, added office space)?

Noninstructional Expenses

Some critics of high levels of spending in higher education focus on noninstructional expenditures. They may be concerned about "administrative bloat"[7] (see box on page 104) or about institutions (particularly in the for-profit sector) spending too much on advertising.[8] After thinking about the best way to hold institutions accountable for the quality of education they offer, some policy advocates have proposed penalizing institutions that spend less than a specified share of their revenues on instruction.[9]

A quarter of postsecondary institutions spend less than 41 percent of their revenues on instruction; a quarter spend more than 71 percent. The median ratio ranges from about 33 percent at for-profit institutions to 64 percent at private nonprofit four-year institutions, but there is also considerable variation within sectors.[10]

Unfortunately, the data on spending patterns that the federal government keeps track of nationally are not very detailed. So, for example, the category "instructional spending" (see explanation in chapter 3) is tightly tied to the activities of classroom (or in some cases online) teaching and the support of those activities. Colleges that spend more dollars on instructional spending tend to have stronger student outcomes, but it does not appear that directing a larger fraction of the total budget to the instructional category necessarily leads to better results.[11] We suspect that one reason for this finding is that many kinds of spending that help students succeed are not included in the instructional budget.

Student support services, like academic and psychological counseling, mentoring, student life programs in dormitories, and others are often of considerable value. Spending on student services can significantly improve persistence and graduation rates, particularly among students most at risk of not completing their programs.[12] Researchers have found that just cutting tuition or giving students more money does not have as strong an impact as providing them with additional support services.[13] In the same vein, commuter colleges often do well to help students solve their transportation challenges, make quiet places for study and group work available, and provide schedule flexibility for students who work.

If the goal is preserving the spending most integral to the institutional mission, careful analysis of both personnel costs and other funds may well lead to decisions different from those arising from the simple dichotomy between instructional and noninstructional costs. Institutions should carefully examine their spending patterns, attempting to analyze which programs are particularly important for student success.

Questions to ask:

- How have expenditures in different areas of the college and on different activities changed in recent years? Are there good explanations for these changes?
- Has anyone on campus carefully studied the impact of staff and services outside the classroom?
- How important is maintaining/increasing the share of enrolling students who stay to complete their degrees?
- Are there good alternatives to the current structure of support systems that might save money without significantly diminishing effectiveness?

What about the Endowment?

As discussed in detail in chapter 8, only a few colleges and universities can cover a significant share of their operating budgets with income from endowments. Still, headlines like the one at the beginning of the chapter about Harvard lead to obvious questions about why, at least in a temporary crisis, the institution cannot simply withdraw a larger-than-usual share of the endowment's returns to plug holes in the budget.

Questions to ask:

- How big is the institution's endowment, both in total and per student?
- What share of the institution's annual spending is covered by the annual payout of the endowment?
- How does the endowment compare to those at similar institutions, and how has it changed over time?
- How much debt does your institution have, and how does that affect its wealth relative to other institutions with similar endowments?
- What share of the endowment is restricted to narrowly specified purposes?
- How is the amount of endowment income added to the operating budget determined each year? How does that amount respond to changes in the value of the endowment? How does it respond to temporary changes in circumstances—such as a pandemic—and to long-term changes—such as declining enrollments or net tuition revenues?

Some Spending Cuts May Come at a High Cost

Comparing different spending plans is not always straightforward. Some expenditures are investments that pay off over time. Education is an obvious example. Paying for college (and foregoing wages to devote time to studying and learning) leaves students financially behind for a while. But it doesn't take too long before the average college graduate overtakes the average high school graduate who went straight to work, with the earnings premium far outweighing the initial investment cost (including both the direct costs and the opportunity cost.). This is an example of how spending in the short-term can strengthen the long-term financial position.

Before advocating cuts in institutional spending on financial aid and student support systems, it is worth considering a parallel example. The City University of New York implemented an experimental program called the Accelerated Study in Associate Programs (ASAP) to improve completion rates for associate degree students facing multiple hurdles to college success. Because the program had such a dramatic effect on completion rates, it lowered the cost per degree despite the substantial investment required to operate the program. Evaluation of the program showed that it is possible to lower the cost per outcome achieved even while increasing total costs.

CUNY spent about $16,300 more on each ASAP student than on students receiving the usual services. Total expenditures rose considerably. But because the share of students earning a degree almost doubled, the cost per degree earned was about 11 percent lower for ASAP students than for students not in the program.[14]

It's not immediately clear how this success affected CUNY's bottom line. The institution (and the state) could decide that they simply cannot afford to offer the kind of programs and services necessary to help their students succeed. But this information should certainly give those committed to the institution's mission pause before advocating budget cuts that might save money today.

This example highlights the importance of carefully considering the long-run implications of any budget cuts on the table.

Administrative Bloat?

Discussions of the rising price of college, as well as faculty concerns over institutional priorities, frequently focus on the idea of "administrative bloat." The suggestion is that colleges and universities are hiring more and more administrators—deans, vice presidents, etc.—raising costs and diminishing the resources available for instruction.

Examples of headlines pointing to this issue include:

"Stop Feeding the College Bureaucratic Bloat"[15]

"Administrative Bloat Meets the Coronavirus Pandemic"[16]

"College administrative bloat is robbing our children of their futures"[17]

No doubt there are examples of universities going overboard with hiring and compensating administrators, but anecdotes are not sufficient to confirm patterns and trends. It is difficult to evaluate the

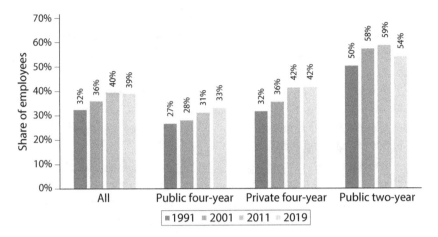

Share of Employees at Degree-Granting Institutions Who Are Faculty
Members, 1991 to 2019
Source: US Department of Education, *Digest of Education Statistics 2020*, Table 314.20

situation without data. And interpreting available data requires some
thought.

According to the Integrated Postsecondary Education Data system,
through which the federal government collects data from all colleges
and universities participating in federal financial aid programs, the
share of college and university employees who are faculty members
has not declined over time. For example, at private four-year colleges it
rose from 32 percent in 1991 to 42 percent in 2011 and 2019.

But even if the share of employees not involved in instruction has
not increased, the share of the budget devoted to these employees
could rise. It turns out, as we noted earlier, that over time, secretaries
and other support staff have been replaced by professional staff—
information technology experts, diversity coordinators, people in
charge of overseeing institutional handling of sexual harassment and
assault claims, psychologists, financial aid professionals, learning
disability experts, and more.

These professional staff, while frequently earning less than they
might in the private sector, are paid more than traditional support
staff. As a result, expenditures on compensation for noninstructional
staff have gone up as a share of most institutions' budgets.

There are good reasons for hiring many of these staff members.
Government regulation of colleges and universities has increased

over time.[18] An increasingly diverse student body in terms of age
and academic preparation in addition to race and ethnicity requires
support services that were less necessary when college access was
more limited. And parent and student expectations combined
with competition among institutions leads to more focus on career
assistance, athletic opportunities, and other services. Moreover, some
of the advising that was the responsibility of the faculty is now in the
hands of dedicated professionals.

The executive-level positions that the phrase "administrative
bloat" conjures up represent a small share of jobs on campus. And as
discussed in more detail above, noninstructional staff are critical to the
college's mission and to student success. Nonetheless, probing more
deeply into the composition of the college staff and changes in overall
compensation expenditures is critical to understanding the financial
circumstances of the institution and the options for change.

CHAPTER SEVEN

Can Pricing and Financial Aid Policies Be More Transparent?

The president of a very selective public university stayed awake rethinking the day's contentious meeting of the admissions and financial aid committees. In a somewhat unusual pattern, the disagreement was not between faculty and administrators. Instead, the Director of Financial Aid, an active participant in his national association with a deep commitment to educational opportunity for state residents, argued that the practice of making large "merit" awards to students with high test scores had to end. These students came disproportionately from affluent white families and had attended the state's best high schools. They were choosing between State U and selective East Coast colleges. The institutional aid they were receiving would not change their lives. Their mostly affluent parents would become a little better off. They would get a great education regardless. But because of the dollars directed to them, the university was forced to scrimp on need-based aid. Students from low-income families were told they would have to borrow the maximum allowed from the federal government and even so, their aid packages would leave gaps of several thousand dollars between what they could afford to pay and what they would have to come up with.

This argument convinced the faculty representative from the Economics Department, who made an impassioned plea for more need-based aid. The mission of the university was to provide the best possible educational opportunities to the state's citizens, and the aid policies were forcing talented low-income students to turn down State U for their local community colleges.

But his colleague from the Chemistry Department protested that if they couldn't enroll the state's highest-achieving students, they would produce fewer science majors, attract less stellar faculty, and lose their status as one of the nation's leaders in graduating future scientists. Merit aid was critical to the future of the institution and the state.

The CFO chimed in, acknowledging the validity of the arguments made by the Director of Financial Aid, but expressing concern about the bottom line. A student from a higher-income family lured to campus with a $5,000 merit award was not going to leave the university just because that award did not increase each year. But a student who needed the $5,000 need-based award to be able to make ends meet would probably need more money each year to continue to pay the bills, as the tuition, fees, room, and board became more expensive. So, the merit scholarship bought the institution more than the need-based scholarship did.

The President of course saw both sides of the argument. In her heart, she was deeply committed to need-based aid and educational opportunity. But she couldn't help imagining a decline in the school's U.S. News rating as they lost high-scoring students, and demands from state legislators to explain declines in net tuition revenues.

THE PRICING SYSTEM for higher education is far from transparent. As discussed in chapter 3, almost all institutions—but particularly public and private nonprofit four-year colleges and universities— charge different prices to different students because some or all students receive price discounts, otherwise known as institutional grant aid or scholarships. Even the full sticker price is sometimes hard to figure out because it consists of a combination of tuition and fees, some of which are required of all students and others of which apply only to some students. Some institutions charge different prices depending on year or field of study. Some have a fixed price for full-time students, usually those enrolled for 12 or more credit hours. Others charge by the credit hour, so students taking 15 hours pay more than those taking 12 hours. A few small residential colleges don't separate room and board charges from tuition and fees, just citing a "comprehensive fee."

Debates about the basic pricing structure usually happen only occasionally. The college may consider promising new students that their tuition will not rise for four years. Or it may consider a dramatic cut in the published price in the hope of reducing sticker shock or gaining some eye-catching news coverage. The idea of switching to a fixed price for full-time students regardless of number of credit hours might be part of efforts to increase on-time completion rates. But only the rate of increase in the price is a standard component of annual budget discussions.

In contrast, debates about financial aid occur consistently because aid is a large component of the annual expenditure budget and because each year there are new students, for whom enrollment decisions might depend on their aid packages, and new opportunities to tweak the aid allocation system.

Background on Financial Aid

Financial aid serves multiple purposes. Many students cannot afford to pay tuition and living expenses, even with all the assistance their families might be able to provide. For them, financial aid makes college a realistic possibility. Aid allocated based on financial circumstances is usually called "need-based" aid. Some of this aid might be in the form of loans, but it is grant aid—dollars that do not have to be repaid—that helps students most. Most grant aid from the federal government comes through the Pell Grant program, a need-based program that supports low- and moderate-income students. Some states provide only need-based based aid, but others base their aid on high school academic achievement ("merit" aid) or on a mix of criteria.

Institutions also use a range of criteria to allocate their grant aid. They use need-based aid to increase the socioeconomic diversity of their student bodies and to further their mission of providing educational opportunities to qualified students. They know that many of the recipients simply could not enroll without institutional grant aid.

But they use other aid dollars to attract athletes, to convince students with strong academic credentials to enroll, or just to be sure they can fill their classes and get enough tuition revenue to operate successfully. For the most part, individual universities and colleges have considerable discretion over how and to whom they award aid, and in fact efforts to coordinate policies or practices across campuses may raise antitrust issues. By contrast, financial aid to athletes has been tightly regulated by the National Collegiate Athletic Association (NCAA). One class of institutions (Division III schools) are forbidden from taking athletic prowess into account in awarding aid, while Division I schools are allotted fixed numbers of grants-in-aid in particular sports, with stringent regulation of the size of awards they can give. This system has come under considerable stress in recent years given the incongruity of a system that aims to protect athletes' amateur status by preventing them from profiting from their performance while at the same time providing coaches with compensation that is orders of magnitude higher than that of presidents and top professors.

Many institutions struggle with the appropriate balance between need-based and non-need-based aid. Some highly selective institutions with ample endowments provide only need-based aid. They have no problem attracting all the highly qualified students for whom they have space. They choose to spend on financial aid so they can enroll the students they most want, regardless of their ability to pay.

Some other institutions cannot fill their classes if they do not provide discounts to a significant share of students. Financial aid is not really a discretionary expenditure for them, because without it, they would have a smaller class and less tuition revenue. These are not dollars they could spend on faculty salaries or technology because there are not enough students willing and able to pay the full tuition price. In some cases, institutions must choose between offering more need-based aid to avoid turning away qualified students with limited ability to pay or offering non-need-based aid to try to attract students with higher test scores who can afford to pay but might choose another school unless they are offered a scholarship.

In 2017–18, almost three-quarters of full-time students at private nonprofit four-year colleges and universities received institutional grant aid: 44 percent received need-based aid, and 51 percent received non-need-based aid. (These add up to more than the total number of recipients because some students received both types of institutional grants.) At public four-year institutions, 41 percent received institutional grants; 13 percent of full-time students at public two-year colleges received this type of aid. At public institutions, the share receiving non-need-based grants also exceeded the share receiving need-based grants.[1]

At all types of institutions, dependent students are more likely than independent students (who are age 24 or older, married, veterans, or for some other reason not considered financially dependent on their parents) to receive institutional grants. Need-based aid goes disproportionately to students from lower-income families, but this is not the case for non-need-based aid.

At four-year institutions, somewhat larger shares of lower-income than of higher-income students receive institutional aid. At private nonprofit colleges and universities, 87 percent of students from families with incomes below $90,000 and 72 percent of those from higher-income families received this aid in 2017–18. At public four-year institutions, these shares were 49 percent and 36 percent, respectively (see table 7.1).

Ability to Pay versus Willingness to Pay

With financial aid, different students pay different prices for the same educational experience on the same college campus. Charging consumers different prices for the same product is not uncommon. As we noted in chapter 2, economists call this practice "price discrimination"—perhaps an unfortunate term. Some people are willing and able to pay a higher price than others for the same product. Some people will walk away if the price goes up; others are less sensitive to price changes.

Some prices differ across groups. Senior citizens pay less than others for movie tickets. Business travelers who book at the last minute pay higher prices for airplane tickets. But because colleges have access to detailed information about both the academic backgrounds and the financial circumstances of applicants, they can adjust prices for individual students.

Table 7.1. Need-Based and Non-Need-Based Institutional Grant Aid, 2017–18

	Any institutional grant		Need-based		Non-need-based	
	Percent receiving	Average award	Percent receiving	Average award	Percent receiving	Average award
	Private Nonprofit Four-Year					
All	74%	$21,422	46%	$16,832	53%	$15,568
Dependency status						
Dependent student	81%	$22,305	51%	$17,310	58%	$16,117
Independent student	38%	$12,137	19%	$10,528	27%	$9,581
Dependent students: Parents' income						
Less than $35,000	85%	$23,122	62%	$18,108	59%	$14,250
$35,000–$79,999	90%	$24,726	66%	$18,585	65%	$15,517
$80,000–$129,999	79%	$22,274	47%	$15,670	58%	$16,919
$130,000 or more	75%	$19,720	37%	$15,609	53%	$17,125
	Public Four-Year					
All	42%	$5,799	20%	$4,835	28%	$5,372
Dependency status						
Dependent student	44%	$5,915	20%	$4,846	29%	$5,500
Independent student	30%	$4,795	17%	$4,755	16%	$4,001
Dependent students: Parents' income						
Less than $35,000	47%	$5,456	30%	$4,677	26%	$4,577
$35,000–$79,999	51%	$5,708	30%	$4,916	29%	$4,841
$80,000–$129,999	41%	$6,169	13%	$4,867	31%	$5,940
$130,000 or more	37%	$6,495	8%	$5,180	32%	$6,428
	Public Two-Year					
All	13%	$2,170	4%	$1,406	10%	$2,333
Dependency status						
Dependent student	14%	$2,344	4%	$1,432	11%	$2,480
Independent student	11%	$1,590	5%	$1,355	6%	$1,674
Dependent students: Parents' income						
Less than $35,000	12%	$2,169	4%	$1,166	9%	$2,465
$35,000–$79,999	15%	$2,137	4%	$13,611	12%	$2,240
$80,000–$129,999	14%	$2,738	3%	$2,198	12%	$2,694
$130,000 or more	15%	$2,454	3%	$1,141	13%	$2,646

Source: US Department of Education (2018), *National Postsecondary Student Aid Study-Administrative Collection*. Calculations by the authors.

For some students, ability to pay determines college choices. For others, the issue is more preferences and priorities, or willingness to pay. The idea that students should get scholarships to State U because otherwise they might prefer another institution is quite different from the idea that students eager to enroll should get scholarships because they do not have the means to pay on their own. One issue is the idea that significantly limiting educational opportunities for those with the most limited resources is inequitable. Another issue is that institutions can influence preferences in a variety of ways. They can improve their curriculum, offer research opportunities, or spruce up their dorms to become desirable to students. But there is no substitute for dollars in ensuring that lower-income students can enroll.

Yet many institutions feel compelled to engage in strategic pricing. A small discount labeled a merit scholarship might attract a student from an affluent family. It might cost much more to enroll a low-income student. At many small private nonprofit colleges, all or almost all students get institutional grant aid, with the idea that people really like to feel they are getting a discount or to believe that the institution is particularly eager for them to enroll.

Colleges Must Make Hard Choices

There is no easy answer to the balancing act required in using institutional grant dollars to meet the multiple goals of increasing access and diversity, filling the class with the highest quality students possible, and ensuring financial stability. Many colleges and universities have found merit-based scholarships to be an effective tool for improving the academic profile of the student body or for increasing enrollments and/or net tuition revenues. The potential effectiveness of such a strategy on a particular campus depends on a variety of factors, including selectivity, the percentage of the applicant pool currently being accepted, and the percentage of those accepted who enroll. The number of students currently receiving institutional grant aid and the discount rate (discussed in detail in chapter 3)—the percentage of gross tuition revenues being offered as grant aid—are also relevant.

Like most firms engaged in price competition, colleges that lower their prices for desirable students find that their competitors are forced to follow suit. This generates a cycle of price cutting for students with particular characteristics—high SAT scores or athletic performance, for example. This price cutting cannot significantly increase the overall supply of students in these categories. As more and more institutional aid dollars are devoted to these students, fewer resources will be available for other priorities, including need-based aid for qualified students who cannot afford to enroll.

Financial Aid versus Other Spending

Some institutions have a strong enough demand for their services that they could fill their classrooms with students willing to pay a high price. This leaves them in the happy position of being able to choose whether to spend some of this available revenue to go after students they especially want, either for purposes of social equity or to meet other goals like staffing the college's student orchestra well. (Athletics is in a special category because what colleges can do to recruit athletes is tightly regulated by the NCAA.) Or, instead of choosing to spend more on student aid, they can devote those dollars to faculty salaries, new technology, or additional student advisors.

However, for other institutions, even if financial aid is a line in the expenditure budget, these choices are not available. Instead of subtracting financial aid, along with other expenditures, from gross revenues calculated as the sticker price times the number of students, they should think about net revenues as the starting point. They must discount the price for some students to convince them to enroll. They would have $0 in revenue from these students if they insisted on charging them the sticker price. Financial aid in these cases is not really an expenditure. It is a pricing strategy aimed at increasing the college's revenue.

Need-Based versus Non-Need-Based Aid

It is easy to think of dollars spent on financial aid for students who could afford to enroll without it as dollars taken out of the pockets of low-income students. This is sometimes the case—but not always. Suppose college A has a tuition price of $20,000. A $5,000 grant makes the difference between Melanie enrolling at A or choosing college B. If Melanie does not enroll, this seat will be empty (or will be filled by a different student with a similar discount). The additional $15,000 in revenue she brings, compared to an empty seat, could fund an extra low-income student—or some other expenditure.

It is not easy to know if that $5,000 scholarship really made the difference for Melanie. It is possible that if the college offered $2,000 scholarships instead and spent a little more on landscaping, more students would fall in love with the campus. It is also possible that the financial aid consultant the college has hired to help them predict which students will enroll under what circumstances cannot really make the precise judgments he claims. If the college follows his suggestion for $5,000 scholarships, it will never know if students would have enrolled with $2,000 scholarships—or with no scholarships at all. The consultant may have shied away from suggesting $2,000, knowing that it would be quite visible if that offer was too low to be effective—but not visible if it was higher than necessary.

But many institutions set aside a fixed amount for financial aid and either turn away low-income students or "gap" those they accept, awarding them less aid than they need to make paying for college a realistic possibility. Among those that reject a significant share (less than 10 percent of all institutions and less than 20 percent of private nonprofit four-year institutions accept less than half of their applicants),[2] a small number—primarily highly selective colleges and universities with large endowments—are "need blind." They accept the most qualified/desirable candidates without regard to their ability to pay. Most of these institutions— as well as a number of those who are need-aware, rejecting some candidates because of their financial need, promise to "meet need." In other words, they ensure that the combination of grants, federal loans, and work-study will fill the gap between the amount the student and family can contribute and the student's budget.

The concepts of being "need blind" and of "meeting need" are flexible in practice. Some institutions declare themselves need blind even if they weigh need in considering transfer students or international students. And it is very different for a college to "meet full need" by limiting recommended student borrowing to, say, $5,000 per year, than to include a $10,000 per year loan for some students.

The difficulties students have financing college education and the reasonable concerns about levels of student debt make a focus on need-based aid critical. Asking about the trade-offs in the financial aid budget is vital at all institutions.

Summary

On every campus, it is important for participants in policy conversations to understand the pricing and financial aid practices in place. Optimal policies differ depending on institutional circumstances. But it is always reasonable to ask if the college is awarding aid to students who can afford to pay while turning students away because of their financial need or leaving accepted students with big resource gaps they will struggle to fill, and if so, what the arguments for this strategy are.

Pricing and aid are policy tools for both ensuring financial stability and creating access and opportunity. Understanding trade-offs, being clear about the role of financial aid in ensuring access and success for students from households with the most limited resources, and considering what changes might be both equitable and efficient should always be on the agenda.

Questions members of all college communities should ask include:

1. What share of undergraduate students at my institution receive institutional grant aid?
2. Does my institution give both need-based and non-need-based institutional grant aid? What is the balance between the two? How do the characteristics of the students receiving each type of aid differ?
3. What would the risks be if we decided to try cutting back on non-need-based aid?
4. How do the average net prices paid by low-income students compare to those paid by those from higher-income households on my campus?
5. How does the share of low-income students (probably estimated as the share of students receiving federal Pell Grants) compare with similar institutions?
6. How many students at my institution leave without completing their programs? How do completion rates compare

for those receiving need-based grants, those receiving non-need-based grants, and those not receiving institutional aid?

7. Does the institution use an external consultant to help make decisions about allocating financial aid? If so, how transparent is the consulting firm about the data and analyses that ground its recommendations?

Tuition and Financial Aid: Beyond the Numbers

In an effort to push colleges to increase financial aid and lower the prices they charge low- and moderate-income students, some public policy proposals would reward increased spending on financial aid.[3] It sounds helpful to encourage increased spending on financial aid, but the numbers can be misleading.

Suppose a college charges tuition of $30,000 and has a discount rate of 40 percent, providing an average of $12,000 per student in financial aid. To meet the demand for more financial aid, the institution raises tuition by $2,000, but also increases each student's aid by $2,000. All students pay the same price as before the change.

The college can now announce that it has increased its spending on financial aid. The new financial aid budget accounts for a larger share of the institution's spending. The discount rate—financial aid dollars as a share of gross tuition revenues—has increased from 40 percent to 44 percent. The numbers suggest an increase in support for students, but they are misleading.

Increases in student aid do not necessarily reduce the prices students pay.

	Original	New
Tuition	$30,000	$32,000
Aid per student	$12,000	$14,000
Net price (tuition—aid per student)	$18,000	$18,000
Discount rate (financial aid/ sticker tuition price)	40%	44%

Source: Simulation by the authors.

Colleges sometimes attempt to soften the news of tuition increases by pointing out that they are increasing financial aid by the same percentage. Although such a move will maintain the discount rate—the share of tuition returned in the form of financial aid—it will increase aid—which is smaller than tuition—by fewer dollars per student. The average net price will rise.

In the table above the $2,000 increase in tuition represents a 6.7 percent increase. The $2,000 increase in financial aid that held students harmless represents a 16.7 percent increase.

If the institution provides grant aid to only half its students, the $800 increase in grant aid per student resulting from a 6.7 percent increase in financial aid would mean a $1,600 increase in aid per recipient. As the table below illustrates, this would still be smaller than the $2,000 tuition increase. Moreover, the increase in sticker price would likely increase the number of students unable to pay the full bill without assistance.

Increasing financial aid and tuition by the same percentage is likely to increase the prices aided student pay.

	Original	6.7% increase	16.7% increase
Tuition	$30,000	$32,000	$35,000
Aid per student	$12,000	$12,800	$14,000
Net price	$18,000	$19,200	$21,000
Discount rate	40%	40%	40%

Source: Simulation by the authors.

Again, the numbers can be misleading. What is the lesson to take away? Look carefully at the pricing and aid data and interpret them with care! One piece of advice: in general, it is usually more constructive to think about net tuition revenue than to fuss with discount rates.

The Strange Reality of Tuition Pricing

Headlines about the high and rising price of college abound. But the reality is that in addition to federal and state grant aid—much of which targets students who are unable to pay on their own—that helps students pay these prices, colleges themselves discount the price for a large share of students.

At many institutions, virtually all students receive institutional grant aid. This practice is most common at small, less selective private nonprofit colleges. In other words, essentially no one pays the published tuition price. How can this make sense?

The retail sector gives some clues. A great many people probably have a pile of coupons from Bed Bath and Beyond stashed away. Some people surely go to the store without their coupons and pay the full price. But no one has to.

The story of JC Penney has become a classic. In 2012, the new CEO decided to get rid of "fake" pricing—to lower prices significantly and abandon the idea of constant sales. It was a disaster.[4] It turns out people are drawn to discounts.

A "price anchor" is a price customers can refer to when making decisions. If the seller can get a higher price into people's heads, they will feel like they are getting a bargain when the price they pay is lower. No one wants to pay the sticker price for a car. They feel better if the salesperson agrees to slash the price for them. Similarly, students and families love getting a letter saying the college values them so much they are offering a scholarship. Paying $30,000 for a $40,000 education sounds like a much better deal than paying $30,000 for a $30,000 education.

Bed Bath and Beyond and JC Penney can effectively advertise their discounts. It is harder for colleges to get the word out that if you enroll, you will get a bargain. From the time Muskingum University garnered considerable attention in 1996 for lowering its price from $14,000 to $10,000, more than a handful of colleges have followed suit, announcing deep tuition price cuts in an effort to attract students who might be scared off by "sticker shock." Some do see big increases in applications, which may or may not last for long. Schools not looking for lots of additional students don't stand to benefit much. And frequently, no students end up paying less—they just get less institutional grant aid.

Observers have questioned for years whether the college pricing model can last. So far, there is no end in sight.

CHAPTER EIGHT

What Is the Role of College Endowments?

THE COLLEGE'S SAVINGS ACCOUNT

In the early days of the coronavirus pandemic, with all the students sent home, the private university's administration was reeling from the financial challenges that compounded the health and safety concerns it faced. It was clear that a significant share of room and board revenues would have to be refunded to the students who had been sent home from campus. The costs of transitioning to virtual learning were mounting. Lots of structural changes were needed to reduce the risk of virus transmission on campus for the people who had to remain there.

Consulting with the chair of the board of trustees, the president and CFO had concluded that the best course of action would be to institute a hiring freeze, cancel salary increases for the coming year, and reduce the share of salaries the university contributed to employee retirement plans.

Now, faculty activists were up in arms. With an endowment of $1 billion, quite a large "nest egg" compared to the typical institution, couldn't the university temporarily increase its draw to supplement the operating budget instead of taking these dollars out of the pockets of struggling faculty and staff? Wasn't the purpose of an endowment to have a cushion in case of an unexpected crisis? Shouldn't the costs of the

*pandemic be spread out over time rather than dumped almost entirely
on the current campus community?*

*Was there any chance of finding some common ground on these
hard questions when the only available communication channels were
Email, text, and Zoom?*

COLLEGE ENDOWMENTS get a lot of attention and spark a lot
of debates. Journalists, members of Congress—and some faculty
members—seem to think that most colleges and universities are
sitting on huge piles of cash that they could easily spend to make
college more affordable—and to raise salaries. But the reality is that
only a few institutions have accumulated significant resources, and
even then, there are frequently a lot of constraints on how they can
use those funds.

What is an endowment? Why do colleges have them? Which
schools have sizeable endowments, and how are they used?

The finances of colleges and universities, especially those that are
private and nonprofit, in many ways look more like those of super-
sized households than like those of private for-profit businesses.
The basic idea of a for-profit business is to make a product or
provide a service for which people will pay more than it costs to
produce and deliver. The difference between costs and revenues is
the profit, which becomes the property of the business's owners.
But nobody owns a nonprofit university, and those who govern it
are not allowed to profit from it. If a college takes in more money
(whether in tuition or in gifts) than it spends, the difference belongs
to the institution.

This is similar to the way family finances work. If the family's
members, through their earnings from work and returns from
investment, bring in more money than they spend, the difference belongs to the family, and it becomes the family's savings.
If the family consistently earns more every year than it spends,
its savings grow, and may be used to buy a house or a car or other
durable asset or may go into a savings account or other financial
investment. When the heads of a family die, usually their accumulated savings are passed on to their children (minus any bequest
taxes).

Putting aside a good many complications (a few of which we will address), this is also how private nonprofit college finances work. In rough terms, a college's accumulated savings are its endowment. When the college's revenues exceed its expenses, the difference can go into the endowment. (This story is a better fit for private nonprofit than for public colleges. Public institutions are owned by the states that operate them, and any excess revenues they generate belong in the first instance to the state. We will say more about public university endowments below.) And in those years when the college spends more than it takes in, the difference comes out of the endowment. A college that has been around for a long time and has consistently pulled in more than it has spent may have quite a large "savings account." It's not surprising that most universities and colleges with very large endowments are very old; some of the wealthiest were founded before the United States. Of course, sometimes a college is "born rich" thanks to a very wealthy donor or a stroke of remarkable luck; in different ways Stanford University, Pomona College, and Olin College are examples.

The reality is, though, that most colleges, like most families, have relatively modest savings accounts. A handful of families possess "dynastic wealth" of either older (Whitney, Rockefeller) or more recent (Bezos, Gates) vintage, but most do not. In fact, a lot of American families have little or no—or even negative—asset accumulation. A very small fraction of families—certainly fewer than 1 percent—can rely on the returns from investing their accumulated savings to provide a major proportion of their livelihood; most people must work for a living.

Just so, most private colleges rely principally on the earnings they get from tuition, room and board, and (to a lesser degree) current giving, mostly from alumni, to pay the bills. The set of institutions that can cover a major portion of their operating expenses from their endowment earnings is quite small. Most colleges just can't save much and, as with households, an unsettlingly large number have negative asset balances—they owe more than they own in financial assets. And even for colleges with sizeable endowments, debt is an important consideration. Two institutions with similar endowments are in very different circumstances if one has preserved its endowment by accumulating a large amount of debt, while at the other, the endowment is a reliable measure of net wealth.

Only a Few Colleges Have Large Endowments

At the end of the 2019–20 academic year, US colleges and universities held endowment assets totaling more than $600 billion. About a quarter of these assets belong to five private research universities. And four public university systems are on the list of the 10 largest endowments. So, a few highly selective, wealthy institutions can take enough income out of their endowments each year to approximately match their tuition revenues. But for the vast majority of colleges and universities, endowments can, at best, provide a small but welcome supplement to the operating budget.

Because enrollment levels range widely in higher education, endowment sizes give limited insight into how much of a typical student's education is supported by the endowment. If we look at endowment per student instead, we learn that Harvard's $41 billion—by far the largest endowment—amounts to more than $1.6 million per student—enough to yield an economic return of about $80,000 per student annually. Princeton, with fewer students and about $27 billion in endowment, has more than double Harvard's per student endowment. Meanwhile, a poorly endowed college may have a resource of only $1,000 per student (or less), which will avail only about $50 toward a year's education for each student (see figure 8.1).

There Are Good Reasons for Colleges to Save

Families value their opportunity to build a "nest egg" for a whole set of reasons. One major reason why accumulated assets are valuable to families is as a kind of insurance policy against unexpected difficulties—a job loss, an unexpected illness, a fire, or a pandemic. For a limited number of families, earnings on accumulated assets also serve as a significant source of income that may help a family afford a second home or expensive vacation or even early retirement. Accumulated assets, often derived from an inheritance, allow a few families to achieve a standard of living that is at an entirely

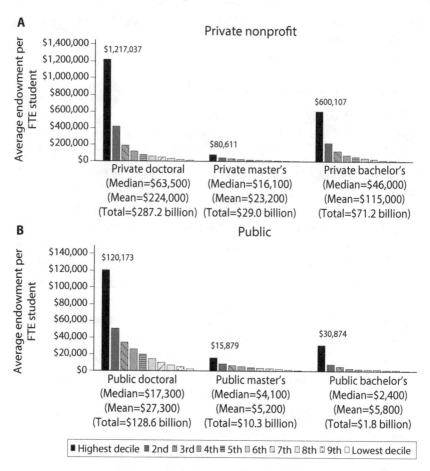

A

Private nonprofit

Average endowment per FTE student

$1,400,000 — $1,217,037
$1,200,000 —
$1,000,000 —
$800,000 —
$600,000 — $600,107
$400,000 —
$200,000 — $80,611
$0 —

Private doctoral
(Median=$63,500)
(Mean=$224,000)
(Total=$287.2 billion)

Private master's
(Median=$16,100)
(Mean=$23,200)
(Total=$29.0 billion)

Private bachelor's
(Median=$46,000)
(Mean=$115,000)
(Total=$71.2 billion)

B

Public

Average endowment per FTE student

$140,000 — $120,173
$120,000 —
$100,000 —
$80,000 —
$60,000 —
$40,000 — $30,874
$20,000 — $15,879
$0 —

Public doctoral
(Median=$17,300)
(Mean=$27,300)
(Total=$128.6 billion)

Public master's
(Median=$4,100)
(Mean=$5,200)
(Total=$10.3 billion)

Public bachelor's
(Median=$2,400)
(Mean=$5,800)
(Total=$1.8 billion)

■ Highest decile ■ 2nd ▨ 3rd ▨ 4th ≣ 5th ▨ 6th ▨ 7th ▨ 8th ▨ 9th □ Lowest decile

FIGURE 8.1. Private Nonprofit and Public Colleges and Universities, 2016–17
Endowment per Student

Notes: Value of endowment assets is as of the end of FY17. Based on data for 189 public doctoral, 255 public master's, 94 public bachelor's, 112 private doctoral, 379 private master's, and 399 private bachelor's institutions. Average endowment per student for each decile is calculated by ordering institutions in the sector by assets per student and dividing the students into deciles. Total assets in institutions enrolling 10 percent of students in the sector are divided by the number of students in those institutions.
Source: College Board (2019), *Trends in College Pricing*, Figure 19

different level from most others. Last, but very important for many American families, is a "bequest motive"—a desire to pass on whatever assets they have been able to accumulate to their children in the hope that their children will enjoy greater economic security and stronger career prospects than they did.

All these motives for saving have their counterparts in the endowment setting. Even a small endowment can help an impecunious college survive a pandemic, a natural disaster, or an economic downturn. For better-funded colleges, an endowment can help them get through a tough year without cutting faculty and staff salaries or financial aid. Better-endowed colleges whose return on assets provides a significant income source can provide a level of amenity to students and faculty that aids in recruiting and also provides real educational benefits.

Colleges, like families, also have a kind of bequest motive. Men and women who found and support colleges and universities almost always envision these institutions as providing benefits to students and to society for an indefinite future. The founders themselves and those who succeed them as trustees tend to have an emotional and even a moral attachment to preserving and enriching the college and therefore its endowment, in addition to a legal obligation. Preservation of the endowment aims to ensure that future students will enjoy at least the same quality of education as today's students. This is a primary motive for building the endowment.

Colleges that seek to build up their assets over time have one big advantage over families: colleges have donors. As nonprofit organizations, colleges can assure would-be donors that their gifts will be used to pursue the college's mission and will not be used to enrich the college's trustees or management. Perhaps less important, donors to colleges can generally receive a tax deduction for their gifts. Many of the most successful colleges and universities devote substantial resources to building positive relations with their alumni and other potential donors and encouraging them to give.

We should be clear that most gifts to a college do not go directly to the college's endowment. Many of them go to fund specific projects or to defray a portion of the college's current operating costs. Other gifts may be earmarked to create and fund a specific program distinct from the college's existing offerings. Still, most gifts wind up being "budget relieving" to a significant extent, and to that extent they can free up resources that can increase the college's savings. A good example is the creation of a "named chair" in a popular department. That chair may well be filled by a distinguished department member. That professor is honored, the donor is pleased, and the college can now shift the salary the professor was already being paid to another purpose.

Decisions about How to Spend from the Endowment May Be Controversial

Struggles over the disposition of a family's wealth lie at the core of many novels and TV series (*Succession*, anyone?), and for the few colleges that have significant assets, questions about the best uses of the endowment drive many discussions. Faculty may want higher salaries and better labs, students may want better fitness centers, and admissions deans may prioritize a new dorm for first-year students or better landscaping. When it comes to the endowment, how much, they want to know, is enough? Chief financial officers and trustees may point to their obligations to future generations of students or emphasize the need to plan for that future rainy day, arguing for accumulation over spending.

Some endowment funds are "restricted." The donors attached requirements that the funds be spent on particular activities. Part of the endowment might be designated for professorships, part of it for need-based financial aid, part of it for training women in science, and part of it for strengthening the business curriculum. However, if the business curriculum is funded partly from the endowment gift and partly from general university funds, there is nothing to stop the university from reducing the general funds going to business and directing that money to hiring faculty in the arts. Because very few activities at universities are fully funded by endowment gifts, even restricted endowments are more "fungible" than they look.

Other endowment funds are "unrestricted" and can be spent as the institution sees fit. Still, the principal must be preserved for future generations. But most endowments include "quasi-endowment" funds. These are funds received by the institution without strings attached requiring that the principal be spent for a specific purpose or preserved in perpetuity. The institution chooses to treat the quasi-endowment funds as though they were given to the endowment. But it can change that choice in the future without violating any laws—as it would if it spent down its true endowment funds.

Most private colleges have a formula that determines how much they spend out of endowment each year—typically referred to as "the draw." The basic idea of most such formulas is to limit spending out of the endowment to a fixed percentage—usually about 4 to 5 percent—of the endowment's value, usually averaged over a few years to prevent the amount of spending from fluctuating too much from year to year. This approach moderates the impact on the dollars flowing from the endowment to the operating budget when the endowment grows dramatically one year because of a sharp rise in financial markets. Faculty and student frustration over what might look like hoarding may be balanced by relief that spending doesn't have to plummet as sharply as it otherwise would when financial markets collapse.

The goal of a spending rate of 4 or 5 percent (see figure 8.2) is to provide some support to the college's budget from endowment growth, but to contain the spending to ensure that the endowment can grow over time. To some degree, different constituencies may debate whether the formula is too generous or too tightfisted.

More common than struggles over the formula that determines the "draw," which can be rather abstract and technical, are arguments about whether and when the college should depart from the formula. These struggles are likely to become intense if, for example, the college endures a sudden drop in its revenues—as the pandemic produced in many places—or a sudden uptick in expenses—as the pandemic also produced. The college will face the prospect of a budget deficit, but formula spending from endowment may be largely unaffected in the near term. Should the college make up the budget gap with extra spending from the endowment (as faculty might prefer) or by sharp budget cuts—salary cuts, layoffs, and such—as spending-conscious trustees or administrators may desire? Even if the endowment grew at the same time the budget gap developed—as was the case for many because of the surprising run-up in the stock market during the pandemic—it may be a few years before the formula will allow increased spending.

Questions of intergenerational equity are part of these debates. Many of the costs of the pandemic had to be borne by current

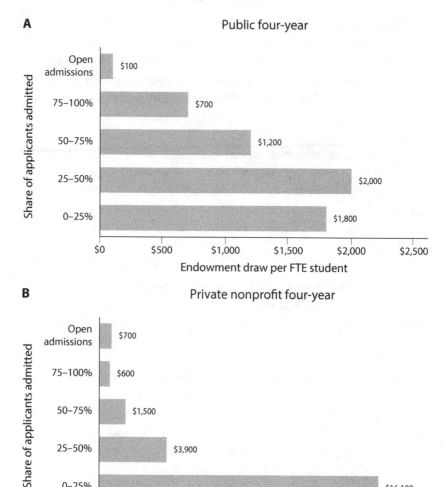

A

Public four-year

B

Private nonprofit four-year

FIGURE 8.2. Average Estimated Endowment Draw per Full-Time Equivalent
Student in Public Four-Year Institutions, Fiscal Year 2015–16
Source: Baum and Lee, *Understanding Endowments*

students, faculty, and staff. The struggles with virtual learning, disease and death, and isolation could not be divided between today and tomorrow. But how should preserving the endowment for the unpredictable crises of the future be weighed against spending more to mitigate suffering today?

Public Institutions

Everything we have said so far applies most directly to nonprofit private colleges and universities. The role of the endowment at public institutions is rather different. (For-profit colleges don't have endowments. They may keep some money on hand to serve as reserves, but any excess revenue a for-profit college earns becomes the property of the owners, who will use it for their own purposes, which may include investing it in the enterprise in search of future profits.) Public universities cannot generally capture excess revenues from their operations as savings that they can keep entirely under their control. Especially if such revenues are large, states may want to recapture them to fund other parts of the state budget. Alternately, states may reduce future state funding to the university, forcing it to spend down the "excess reserves."

The endowments of public colleges are generally overseen by separate nonprofit enterprises often called "foundations." Gifts intended to benefit a public university are generally directed to its foundation and are used by the university for purposes decided by donors and by the foundation's board, generally in close cooperation with the university's leadership. The foundation's assets are not the property of the state. These arrangements are subject to a lot of special cases and local circumstances, but generally public university endowments play more limited and prescribed roles in the university's funding. The University of Texas system has the second largest endowment in the nation, but because its student body is so large, its endowment per student is considerably smaller than those of private institutions with similar endowments. And most public university endowments are much smaller.

In both the public and private sectors, the institutions with endowments that provide significant supplements to their operating budgets tend to be highly selective. For example, public institutions that accept less than a quarter of their applicants average about $1,800 a year per student from the endowment. Those accepting 75 to 100 percent average $700 a year. In the private nonprofit sector, the parallel figures are $16,100 per student and $600 per student. In other words, the institutions whose students face the most significant barriers and who are most likely to struggle with both finances and student outcomes cannot turn to endowments for help. But the more selective, wealthier institutions have more options.

Summary

Campuses with sizeable endowments should have ongoing conversations about the trade-offs between growing the endowment to ensure the institution's future and subsidizing current spending to support the current community. It is easy for trustees and administrators to get caught up in a race to grow the endowment regardless of its current size. It is easy for faculty and staff to resent the sacrifices they see themselves making in the interest of some future unknown institutional need—particularly in times of particular stress on the economy and the college's budget.

Asking questions about how to balance growing the endowment with enhancing current spending is a luxury in which few colleges and universities can join. For most, current revenues from tuition and fees or state appropriations are by far the main concerns. But having a reasonable nest egg is as important for educational institutions as it is for households.

CHAPTER NINE

Conclusion:
Moving Forward

WE MIGHT WISH that campus decision-making and policy setting took place through calm, rational discourse and respectful disagreement. But in reality, disputes about policies or practices on campus are too often marked by dogmatic assertions and mutual suspicion about motives, as well as by misunderstanding of the fundamentals of college finance. There is more than one reason for this. Those engaged with academic institutions, including trustees, faculty, staff, and administrators (as well as students), tend to be passionately attached to the mission of their college or university and believe in fighting for their beliefs—as well as for their own personal well-being.

From their beginnings in the Middle Ages, European and later American universities have been "loosely coupled organizations," where colleges with differing academic specializations were gathered together for administrative purposes. Universities and colleges continue to need to hold together experts in very different subjects under one roof, and are therefore much less hierarchical than typical businesses or government agencies. To a far greater extent than in most other organizations, everybody expects to be heard, and decision-making authority is dispersed, with broad consultation critical to outcomes being accepted.

We wouldn't have it any other way. Yet, valuable as decentralized authority and extensive voice for faculty and other members of the enterprise are, the need to make choices and allocate resources is real. Cooperating on making difficult decisions requires shared language, open communication, knowledge about necessary trade-offs, and respect for differing perspectives and priorities—in addition to shared commitment to the institutional mission.

This book has introduced a set of concepts and vocabulary that we believe provide useful grounding for constructive campus conversations. Another prerequisite for constructive deliberation is a shared grasp on where your institution fits into the larger universe of higher education. One of Teddy Roosevelt's many mottoes was "Do what you can with what you have, where you are." Faculty members who expect their salaries to match those of institutions with much higher endowment per student than their own may frustrate themselves by demanding the impossible. And administrators who expect the same level of research productivity from faculty who have twice the teaching load will risk poor teaching, shoddy research, and terrible morale. We have tried here to provide a sketch of the enormous variety of institutions, with different aims, opportunities, and resources, which dot our nation's landscape. Everybody should want to improve, but ambitions should be grounded in current realities and meaningful opportunities for change.

Readers can build on this foundation to engage with colleagues in deliberations about the challenging choices colleges and universities face in meeting the needs of their students and communities, as well as of the faculty, staff, and administrators who make the place function.

What steps can you take on your campus to apply some of the lessons learned?

We hope this book will inspire participants in shared governance to sit down with their counterparts on campus to plan for improved dialogue. Thinking together with others in different positions with different responsibilities about how to bring campus constituencies together for reasoned exchanges is a first step in setting up a process for educating and incorporating those coming from different starting points.

A core group could agree on a framework, planning a series of conversations that centers on process, the exchange of ideas, and shared conceptual grounding. Instead of waiting for a controversial issue to ignite debate, it would be helpful to generate dialogue about how to approach such issues when they arise.

Sometimes outside facilitators can make conversations like these more productive. The idea is not for the chief financial officer to impart wisdom about resource constraints to the rest of the community—although this is certainly a necessary step in the process. Rather, the idea is to share priorities, reactions to others' language, and concerns about seemingly neglected priorities. Everyone has to be open to learning. All parties to the conversation have much to learn from others.

Another useful step, once the groundwork for dialogue is in place, is to debate some hypothetical issues. Controversies on other campuses that are not likely to arise on your campus can provide opportunities to exchange ideas and hear others' approaches without too much emotional engagement.

Then, when your campus faces a challenge that must be addressed through shared governance—wherever primary responsibility for the decision lies—faculty, staff, administrators, and trustees will be prepared to converse, debate, and discuss the trade-offs involved and the marginal differences likely to result from alternative decisions.

Good luck!!

NOTES

Introduction

1. In addition to being liberal arts college faculty members, one of us (McPherson) served as Dean of the Faculty and President at liberal arts colleges. Each of us has been a member of the Board of Trustees at a private liberal arts college. McPherson has also been a trustee at a public four-year college.

2. Friga (2021), "How Much Has Covid Cost Colleges? $183 Billion," *Chronicle of Higher Education.*

3. National Association of Student Financial Aid Administrators (2021), "Higher Education Emergency Relief Funds Comparison Chart."

4. Washington Center for Equitable Growth (2019), "The Distribution of Wealth in the United States and Implications for a Net Worth Tax."

Chapter 1: Colleges, College Students, and College Finances

1. US Department of Education (2021), *Digest of Education Statistics 2020,* Table 306.50, n.p.

2. College Board, *Trends in College Pricing 2021,* Table CP-12.

3. Bound and Turner, "Cohort Crowding;" Deming and Walters, "Impacts of Price and Spending Subsidies."

4. US Department of Education (2018), *National Postsecondary Student Aid Study-Administrative Collection,* National Center for Education Statistics Data Lab. Calculations by the authors.

5. US Dept. of Education, *National Postsecondary Student Aid Study (NPSAS:16), Student Financial Aid Estimates for 2015–16, First Look,* Table 1.

6. College Board (2021), *Trends in College Pricing 2021,* Tables CP-9 and CP-10.

7. Questions about how high levels of income and wealth inequality affect the operations of colleges and universities, and of the role higher education policies play in influencing the extent of inequality, are a major topic in our recent book, *Can College Level the Playing Field.*

Chapter 2: Basic Economic Concepts and College Financing

1. Academic Anchor, "University Humor: Dwight Eisenhower." Helfand, "Higher Education.".

2. Rohan and Smythe, "PA State System Universities."

Chapter 3: Building Blocks of College Finance

1. National Association of College and University Business Officers, *2020 Tuition Discounting Study*.

2. US Department of Education, *Digest of Education Statistics 2020*, Table 334.10.

3. Lieber (2021), *The Price You Pay for College*, as reported in Gold, "Here's Where Your College Tuition Really Goes."

4. US Bureau of Labor Statistics, "Labor Productivity and Costs."

5. Baum and McPherson, "Human Factor."

6. Fain (2019), "Philosophy Degrees and Sales Jobs."

7. Goldin and Katz, *Race Between Education and Technology*; Autor, Goldin, and Katz, "Extending the Race between Education and Technology."

8. Deming and Noray. "Earnings Dynamics"; Deming, "Growing Importance of Social Skills."

Chapter 4: Is a College a Business?

1. Almost three-quarters of all postsecondary institutions, including 83 percent of public institutions, 49 percent of private nonprofit institutions, and 93 percent of for-profit instructions accept at least 75 percent of their applicants (US Department of Education, *Digest of Education Statistics 2020*, Table 305.40).

Chapter 5: How Should We Think about the Compensation Budget?

1. US Department of Education, *Digest of Education Statistics 2019*, Tables 316.10, 316.70; 2018–19; American Association of University Professors, *AAUP Faculty Compensation Survey*.

2. US Census Bureau, "Current Population Survey Historical Income Tables," Table P-2.

3. Authors' calculation from the Federal IPEDS (Integrated Postsecondary Education System). Data are for fiscal year 2019.

4. American Association of University Professors, *2020–21 Faculty Compensation Survey Results*, Table 5.

5. American Association of University Professors, *2020–21 Faculty Compensation Survey Results*, Table 3.

6. Higher Ed Jobs, *Tenured/Tenure-Track Faculty Salaries*.

7. US Bureau of Labor Statistics, "Employee Benefits in the United States, March 2020."

8. American Association of University Professors, *2020–21 Faculty Compensation Survey Results*, Tables 8 and 9.

9. National Center for Education Statistics, *IPEDS Data Explorer*.

10. Carlin, "Restoring Sanity to an Academic World Gone Mad."

11. TIAA-CREF, "To Retire or Not?

12. US Bureau of Labor Statistics, "Employee Tenure News Release," September 22, 2020.

13. Yildirmaz, Ryan, and Nezaj, *2019 State of the Workforce Report.*

14. McPherson and Schapiro, "Tenure Issues in Higher Education."

15. Yildirmaz and Nezaj, *2019 State of the Workforce Report.*

16. University of Maryland, "Faculty Time Use Study."

17. Chait," Future of Academic Tenure"; Gardner, "Want to Kill Tenure?"

18. College for All Act of 2021, 117th Congress, First Session.

19. American Association of University Professors, *Data Snapshot.*

20. Hearn and Burns, "Contingent Faculty Employment."

21. Baldwin and Wawrzynski, "Contingent Faculty as Teachers."

22. Figlio and Schapiro, "Staffing the Higher Education Classroom."

Chapter 6: Do We Really Have to Cut the Budget?

1. Hubler, "Colleges Slash Budgets in the Pandemic."

2. Flaherty, "College Lower the Boom on Retirement Plans."

3. Kim, "Harvard to Impose a Salary and Hiring Freeze."

4. American Association of University Professors, *2020–21 Faculty Compensation Survey Results.*

5. See, for example Reese, "SCU Employees Frustrated"; Flaherty, "Retirement Benefits Return."

6. Gould, "Working Scientist podcast"; Malloy, Young, and Berdahl, "PhD. Oversupply."

7. Belkin and Thurm, "Deans List."

8. Cellini and Chaudhary, "Commercials for College?"

9. Elliott and Jones, *Creating Accountability for College Access and Success.*

10. Cheslock, *Examining Instructional Spending.*

11. Restrepo and Turner, *Higher Education Performance and Accountability.*

12. Webber and Ehrenberg, "Do Expenditures Other Than Instructional Expenditures Affect Graduation and Persistence Rates."

13. Angrist, Lang, and Oreopoulos, "Incentives and Services for College Achievement"; Deming and Walters, "Impact of Price Caps and Spending Cuts."

14. Scrivener et al, *Doubling Graduation Rates,* 71.

15. Hamburger, "Stop Feeding the College Bureaucratic Bloat."

16. Gross, "Administrative Bloat Meets the Coronavirus Pandemic."

17. Murphy, "College Administrative Bloat."

18. See Vanderbilt University, *The Cost of Federal Regulatory Compliance in Higher Education.*

Chapter 7: Can Pricing and Financial Aid Policies be More Transparent?

1. US Department of Education (2018), *National Postsecondary Student Aid Study-Administrative Collection*. Calculations by the authors.

2. U.S. Department of Education, *Digest of Education Statistics 2020*, Table 305.40

3. See, for example, Reed, "Reducing Excessive Debt."

4. See, for example, Tuttle, "The 5 Big Mistakes."

REFERENCES

Academic Anchor (2012). "University Humor: Dwight Eisenhower." Academic Anchor, https://academicanchor.wordpress.com/2012/08/09/dwight-eisenhower-and -university-faculty/.

American Association of University Professors (2019). *2018–19 AAUP Faculty Compensation Survey. Inside Higher Ed.* Accessed June 2021. https://www.insidehighered .com/aaup-compensation-survey?institution-name=&professor-category=1601.

———. (2021). *2020–21 Faculty Compensation Survey Results.* Accessed April 21, 2021.

———. (n.d.). *Data Snapshot: Contingent Faculty in U.S. Higher Ed.* Accessed May 5, 2021. https://www.aaup.org/news/data-snapshot-contingent-faculty-us-higher-ed.

Angrist, Joshua, Daniel Lang, and Philip Oreopoulos (2009). "Incentives and Services for College Achievement: Evidence from a Randomized Trial," *American Economic Journal: Applied Economics* 1, No. 1: 136–63.

Autor, David, Claudia Goldin, and Lawrence F. Katz. 2020. "Extending the Race between Education and Technology." *AEA Papers and Proceedings.* 110: 347–51.

Baldwin, Roger and Matthew Wawrzynski (2011). "Contingent Faculty as Teachers: What We Know; What We Need to Know." *American Behavioral Scientist* 55, No. 11: 1485–1509.

Baum, Sandy and Victoria Lee (2018). *Understanding Endowments.* Washington, DC: Urban Institute.

Baum, Sandy and Michael McPherson (2019). "The Human Factor: The Promise and Limits of Online Education." *Daedalus* 148, no. 4: 235–54.

———. (2022). *Can College Level the Playing Field? Higher Education in an Unequal Society.* Princeton, NJ: Princeton University Press.

Belkin, Douglas and Scott Thurm (2012, December 28)."Deans List: Hiring Spree Fattens College Bureaucracy—and Tuition," *Wall Street Journal.* https://www.wsj.com /articles/SB10001424127887323316804578161490716042814.

Bhutta, Neil, Andrew Chang, Lisa Dettling, and Joanne Hsu (2020). "Disparities in Wealth by Race and Ethnicity in the 2019 Survey of Consumer Finances." *Fed Notes.* Washington, DC: Board of Governors of the Federal Reserve.

Bound, John and Sarah Turner (2007). "Cohort Crowding: How Resources Affect Collegiate Attainment," *Journal of Public Economics* 91, No. 5–6: 877–99.

Carlin, James (1999, November 5). "Restoring Sanity to an Academic World Gone Mad." *Chronicle of Higher Education*, n.p.

Cellini, Stephanis and Latika Chaudhary (2020). "Commercials for College? Advertising in Higher Education." Washington, DC: Brookings Institution. https:// www.brookings.edu/research/commercials-for-college-advertising-in-higher -education/.

Chait, Richard (1995). "The Future of Academic Tenure." *AGB Priorities* 3.

Cheslock, John (2019). *Examining Instructional Spending for Accountability and Consumer Information Purposes*. New York: The Century Foundation.

Chronicle of Higher Education (2020, August 16). "Percentages of Full-Time Faculty Members Who Were Non-Tenure Track, by Institutional Classification, 2018-19." *The Almanac, 2020-21*. https://www.chronicle.com/article/percentages-of-full-time-faculty-members-who-were-non-tenure-track-by-institutional-classification-2018-19.

College for All Act of 2021, S.R. 1288, 117th Congress, First Session. https://www.sanders.senate.gov/wp-content/uploads/AEG21437-2.pdf.

College Board (2019, 2020, 2021). *Trends in College Pricing*. New York: College Board.

———. (2020). *Trends in Student Aid*. New York: College Board.

Deming, David (2017, November). "The Growing Importance of Social Skills in the Labor Market." *Quarterly Journal of Economics* 132. No. 4: 1593–1640. https://doi.org/10.1093/qje/qjx022.

Deming, David and Kadeem Noray (2020, November)."Earnings Dynamics, Changing Job Skills, and STEM Careers." *Quarterly Journal of Economics* 135, No.4: 1965–2005. https://doi.org/10.1093/qje/qjaa021.

Deming, David and Christopher Walters (2017). "The Impacts of Price and Spending Subsidies on U.S. Postsecondary Attainment," Cambridge, MA: NBER Working Paper 23736.

Elliott, Kayla and Tiffany Jones (2019). *Creating Accountability for College Access and Success: Recommendations for the Higher Education Act and Beyond*. Washington, DC: The Education Trust.

Fain, Paul (2019) "Philosophy Degrees and Sales Jobs." *Inside Higher Ed*. https://www.insidehighered.com/news/2019/08/02/new-data-track-graduates-six-popular-majors-through-their-first-three-jobs.

Figlio, David and Morton Schapiro (2021). "Staffing the Higher Education Classroom." *Journal of Economic Perspectives* 35, No. 1: 143–62.

Flaherty, Colleen (2020, May 21). "Colleges Lower the Boom on Retirement Plans." *Inside Higher Ed*. https://www.insidehighered.com/news/2020/05/21/more-institutions-are-suspending-or-cutting-retirement-plan-contributions.

———. (2021, May 24). "Retirement Benefits Return." *Inside Higher Ed*. https://www.insidehighered.com/news/2021/05/24/most-institutions-are-resuming-or-even-restoring-retirement-benefits-cut-during.

Friga, Paul (2021). "How Much Has Covid Cost Colleges? $183 Billion." *Chronicle of Higher Education*. https://www.chronicle.com/article/how-to-fight-covids-financial-crush.

Gardner, Lee (2018, June 18). "Want to Kill Tenure? Be Careful What You Wish For." *Chronicle of Higher Education*, n.p.

Gold, Howard (2021, January 26). "Here's Where Your College Tuition Really Goes." *Marketwatch*.

Gould, Julie (2019). "Working Scientist Podcast: Too Many PhDs, Too Few Research Positions." *Nature*. https://www.nature.com/articles/d41586-019-03439-x.

Goldin, Claudia and Lawrence Katz (2008). *The Race Between Education and Technology*. Cambridge, MA: Belknap Harvard Press.

Gross, Erik (2020). "Administrative Bloat Meets the Coronavirus Pandemic." *Forum*. https://www.goacta.org/2020/06/administrative-bloat-meets-the-coronavirus-pandemic/.

Hamburger, Philip (2019, June 2). "Stop Feeding the College Bureaucratic Bloat. *Wall Street Journal*, Opinion. https://www.wsj.com/articles/stop-feeding-college-bureaucratic-bloat-11559507310.

Hearn, James and Rachel Burns (2021). "Contingent Faculty Employment and Financial Stress in Public Universities." *Journal of Higher Education* 92 No. 3: 331–62.

Helfand, David (2011). "Higher Education: Academic Questions," *Nature*. https://www.nature.com/articles/477158a.

Higher Ed Jobs (2021). *Tenured/Tenure-Track Faculty Salaries*. Accessed June 2021. https://www.higheredjobs.com/salary/salaryDisplay.cfm?SurveyID=56.

Hubler, Shawn (2021, April 26). "Colleges Slash Budgets in the Pandemic, with 'Nothing Off-Limits,'" *New York Times*. https://www.nytimes.com/2020/10/26/us/colleges-coronavirus-budget-cuts.html.

Kim, Jasmone (2020, April 14). "Harvard to Impose a Salary and Hiring Freeze Due to Fallout from Coronavirus Outbreak." CNBC. https://www.cnbc.com/2020/04/14/harvard-announces-salary-and-hiring-freeze-due-to-coronavirus.html.

Lieber, Ron (2021). *The Price You Pay for College: An Entirely New Roadmap for the Biggest Financial Decision Your Family Will Ever Make*. New York: Harper Collins.

Malloy, Jonathan, Lisa Young and Loleen Berdahl (2021, July 16). "Ph.D. Oversupply: The System is the Problem," *Inside Higher Ed*. https://www.insidehighered.com/advice/2021/06/22/how-phd-job-crisis-built-system-and-what-can-be-done-about-it-opinion.

McPherson, Michael, S., and Morton Owen Schapiro (1999). "Tenure Issues in Higher Education." *Journal of Economic Perspectives* 13, No. 1: 85–98.

Moran, Lawrence (2014). "The Faculty Is the University," *Sandwalk* (blog). https://sandwalk.blogspot.com/2014/05/the-faculty-is-university.html.

Murphy, Greg (2020, December 9). "College Administrative Bloat Is Robbing Our Children of Their Futures." *Washington Examiner*. https://www.washingtonexaminer.com/opinion/op-eds/college-administrative-bloat-is-robbing-our-children-of-their-futures.

National Association of College and University Business Officers (2021). *2020 Tuition Discounting Study*. Washington, DC: NACUBO.

National Association of Student Financial Aid Administrators (2021). "Higher Education Emergency Relief Funds Comparison Chart." https://www.nasfaa.org/uploads/documents/HEERF_Funds_Comparison_Chart.pdf.

Reed, Tom (2018). "Reducing Excessive Debt and Unfair Costs of Education (REDUCE) Act," H. R. 5916, 115th Congress. https://reed.house.gov/news/documentsingle.aspx?DocumentID=1442.

Reese, Madelyne (2021, June 2). "SCU Employees Frustrated, Allege 'Unethical Financial Behavior,' *SanJoseInside*. https://www.sanjoseinside.com/news/scu-employees-frustrated-allege-unethical-financial-behavior/.

Restrepo, Leonardo and Lesley Turner (2012). *Higher Education Performance and Accountability: Insights from a New Visualization Tool.* Washington, DC: Brookings Institution, Hutchins Center on Fiscal and Monetary Policy.

Rohan, Jess and Lauren Smythe (2019, April 4). "Pa. State System Universities to Craft Their Own Tuition Rates Every Two Years." *Philadelphia Inquirer*.

Scrivener, Susan, Michael Weiss, Alyssa Ratledge, Timothy Rudd, Colleen Sommo, and Hannah Fresques (2015). *Doubling Graduation Rates: Three-Year Effects of CUNY's Accelerated Study in Associate Programs (ASAP) for Developmental Education Students*, MDRC. https://www.mdrc.org/sites/default/files/doubling_graduation _rates_fr.pdf.

State Higher Education Executive Officers (2021), State Higher Education Finance Report, FY2020. https://shef.sheeo.org/report/.

TIAA-CREF (1998). "To Retire or Not? Examining Life after the End of Mandatory Retirement in Higher Education." *Research Dialogues* 58. https://www.tiaainstitute .org/sites/default/files/presentations/2017-02/58.pdf.

Tuttle, Brad (2013). "The 5 Big Mistakes That Led to Ron Johnson's Ouster at JC Penney." *Time*. https://business.time.com/2013/04/09/the-5-big-mistakes-that-led-to -ron-johnsons-ouster-at-jc-penney/.

University of Maryland (2017). "Faculty Time Use Study." ADVANCE Program for Inclusive Excellence and Time Use Laboratory. https://www.uww.edu/documents /ir/University-Wide%20Surveys/Faculty%20Time%20Use/FINAL%20Summary %20Report-%20Faculty%20Time%20Study%202017%20Implementation.pdf.

US Bureau of Labor Statistics (2020, September 22). "Employee Tenure News Release." https://www.bls.gov/news.release/archives/tenure_09222020.htm.

———. (2021). "Labor Productivity and Costs." https://www.bls.gov/lpc/prodybar.htm.

———. (2020, September 24). "Employee Benefits in the United States, March 2020" (News Release). https://www.bls.gov/news.release/archives/ebs2_09242020 .pdf#:~:text=EMPLOYEE%20BENEFITS%20IN%20THE%20UNITED%20 STATES%E2%80%93%20MARCH2020%20Paid,reported%20today.%20 %28See%20chart%201%20and%20table%206.%29.

US Census Bureau (2020). "Current Population Survey, Annual Social and Economic Supplement," FINC-03.

———. (2020). "Current Population Survey Historical Income Tables."

———. (2020). "Current Population Survey, Annual Social and Economic Supplement, Educational Attainment in the United States," Table 1.

US Department of Education (2017, 2019, 2020, 2021). *Digest of Education Statistics.* National Center for Education Statistics.

———. (2020). Integrated Postsecondary Education Data System. https://nces.ed.gov /ipeds/.

———. (2020). Integrated Postsecondary Education Data Explorer. https://nces.ed.gov /datalab/

———. (n.d.). *2015–16 National Postsecondary Student Aid Study (NPSAS:16), Student Financial Aid Estimates for 2015–16, First Look.* Accessed June 5, 2021. https://nces.ed.gov/pubs2018/2018466.pdf.

———. (2016). *National Postsecondary Student Aid Study.* Data Lab. National Center for Education Statistics.

———. (2018). *National Postsecondary Student Aid Study-Administrative Collection.* Data Lab. National Center for Education Statistics.

Vanderbilt University (2015). *The Cost of Federal Regulatory Compliance in Higher Education: A Multi-Institutional Study. An Assessment of Federal Regulatory Compliance Costs at 13 Institutions in FY 2013–2014.* https://news.vanderbilt.edu/files/Regulatory-Compliance-Report-Final.pdf.

Washington Center for Equitable Growth (2019). *The Distribution of Wealth in the United States and Implications for a Net Worth Tax.* https://equitablegrowth.org/the-distribution-of-wealth-in-the-united-states-and-implications-for-a-net-worth-tax/.

Webber, Douglas and Ronald Ehrenberg (2010). "Do Expenditures Other Than Instructional Expenditures Affect Graduation and Persistence Rates in American Higher Education?" *Economics of Education Review* 29, No. 6, 947–58.

Yildirmaz, Ahu, Christopher Ryan, and Jeff Nezaj (2019). *2019 State of the Workforce Report: Pay, Promotions and Retention.* Roseland, NJ: ADP Research Institute.

A NOTE ON THE TYPE

THIS BOOK has been composed in Miller, a Scotch Roman typeface designed by Matthew Carter and first released by Font Bureau in 1997. It resembles Monticello, the typeface developed for The Papers of Thomas Jefferson in the 1940s by C. H. Griffith and P. J. Conkwright and reinterpreted in digital form by Carter in 2003.

Pleasant Jefferson ("P. J.") Conkwright (1905–1986) was Typographer at Princeton University Press from 1939 to 1970. He was an acclaimed book designer and AIGA Medalist.